Giving Voice

This book is a practical guide for using the power of theatre to address issues of oppression in areas such as race, ethnicity, LGBTQ+, gender, and sexual harassment.

Giving Voice charts a roadmap for the process of establishing a troupe, including auditioning members, utilizing authentic source material, directing rehearsals, guiding mindful growth among troupe members, and facilitating an inclusive forum environment. Rooted in Augusto Boal's Theatre of the Oppressed and using the nationally recognized Missouri State University's *Giving Voice* troupe as a model, this book provides guidance for customizing the program's principles to meet the needs of your school, community, organization, or business. *Giving Voice* forums bring professional development to a new level. Applications include diversity and cultural awareness training in educational settings for students, staff, faculty, and administrators, as well as those in non-profit and for-profit organizations.

This book provides a powerful and proven approach to creating a truly inclusive climate. It is a guidebook for accessible use in the secondary and university settings in theatre and performance studies. It has also been shown to be effective for businesses and other organizations.

Carol J. Maples is a professor and theatre director at Missouri State University, USA. She is the Director of *Giving Voice*, a nationally recognized interactive theatre troupe that addresses various issues of diversity, oppression, and micro-aggressions. She is recipient of Missouri State University's Foundation Award for Service and an Outstanding Advising Certificate of Merit at the National Academic Advising Association's Global Awards Ceremony.

Routledge Advances in Theatre & Performance Studies

This series is our home for cutting-edge, upper-level scholarly studies and edited collections. Considering theatre and performance alongside topics such as religion, politics, gender, race, ecology, and the avant-garde, titles are characterized by dynamic interventions into established subjects and innovative studies on emerging topics.

Theatre and Human Rights
The Politics of Dramatic Form
Gary M. English

Who Is In the Room?
Queer Strategies for Redefining the Role of the Theater Director
Brooke O'Harra

Arabs, Politics, and Performance
George Potter, Roaa Ali, and Samer Al-Saber

Performing the Transition to Democracy
Theater and Performance in 1970s Spain
David Rodríguez-Solás

Dressaged Animality
Human and Animal Actors in Contemporary Performance
Lisa Moravec

Giving Voice
The Power of Theatre for Positive Change
Carol J. Maples

For more information about this series, please visit: www.routledge.com/Routledge-Advances-in-Theatre–Performance-Studies/book-series/RATPS

Giving Voice

The Power of Theatre for Positive Change

Carol J. Maples

LONDON AND NEW YORK

First published 2024
by Routledge
4 Park Square, Milton Park, Abingdon, Oxon OX14 4RN

and by Routledge
605 Third Avenue, New York, NY 10158

Routledge is an imprint of the Taylor & Francis Group, an informa business

British Library Cataloguing-in-Publication Data
A catalogue record for this book is available from the British Library

ISBN: 9781032676845 (hbk)
ISBN: 9781032676869 (pbk)
ISBN: 9781032676883 (ebk)

DOI: 10.4324/9781032676883

Typeset in Times New Roman
by KnowledgeWorks Global Ltd.

To Gina Wyckoff, whose love, support, and belief in me made doing the work of *Giving Voice* and this book possible.

Contents

Preface

This book is the result of my desire to help others do *Giving Voice* type work in their own environments. I wanted a singular, proven, practical application guide ready for those who want to use theatre to make positive change. I also wanted to honor the work of troupe members over the years who have inspired me with their dedication to making this world better. As *Giving Voice* warriors, they have also inspired and touched the hearts of audience members across the nation as they gave voice to the marginalized.

Acknowledgments

First and foremost, I wish to acknowledge Melissa Herr, who along with her excellent insights, convinced me only I could tell these stories and encouraged me to share this important work. I also must acknowledge my Editor, Laura Hussey, and Editorial Assistant, Swatti Hindwan, for their patience and support in navigating this new endeavor. My appreciation to my doctoral advisor, Barbara Martin, who supported me through my research and dissertation that would become *Giving Voice*. Additionally, I wish to acknowledge Chris Craig, Jill Patterson, and Wes Pratt, whose leadership at Missouri State provided *Giving Voice* invaluable support throughout the university and beyond. My gratitude also goes to Missouri State University and the Department of Theatre and Dance for the time to write this book. Finally, my thanks to Jon Herbert for his care of the *Giving Voice* troupe while I was away.

1 Introduction

Giving Voice

> Growing up, my mom told me I always start ten steps behind because of the color of my skin. Therefore, I must work longer and harder to have a chance of reaching the same finish line. In most of my classes, I am the only one that looks like me. So, I either get ignored, called out for not paying attention when I am actually taking notes, or called on to speak for everyone that looks like me. Yes, I am frustrated but unlike my classmates, if I speak up then I am accused of being 'aggressive' which is code for "angry Black woman"
>
> (*Giving Voice* character)

This insight was shared during a *Giving Voice* performance. After being asked why she shut down in certain situations, the troupe member expressed frustration with having to provide the "Black perspective" when no other students are asked to contribute in this manner. *Giving Voice* is a form of theatre that creates a space where audience members can have meaningful discussions with the characters from a scenario that goes beyond stereotypes and assumptions. The audience gets to know the characters on a personal level, asking questions they might never have the opportunity to ask of someone different from themselves. It is a compelling interaction. To paraphrase Dr. Martin Luther King, Jr., an audience cannot defect from an insight. They cannot unsee what they have seen nor can they unhear what they have heard. This is the power of theatre, and it can be used to make our world a better place.

Interactive theatre training is the basis for Missouri State University's *Giving Voice*, a troupe of university students utilizing a unique and engaging approach to confront oppression and address challenging interpersonal situations. Emphasizing the power of storytelling through various theatre exercises, the *Giving Voice* Project was developed to confront prejudice and stereotypes resulting in oppression, especially microaggressions. This engaging approach opens the often difficult dialogue needed to improve the classroom

DOI: 10.4324/9781032676883-1

or work environment for everyone. The troupe now prefers to describe this as *courageous conversations*.

At the 2006 Association for Theatre in Higher Education conference, I experienced a workshop based on Augusto Boal's *Theatre of the Oppressed*. This powerful presentation gave me the direction I needed for my doctoral research and dissertation. In turn, what I learned about the impact of this type of theatre would inform my professional and personal life for years to come. This interactive form of theatre helps find ways to improve lives, especially the lives of the marginalized. The workshop was developed for faculty to learn more about what their students are experiencing, especially when trying to have significant meetings about their thesis work with graduate advisors who have little time. During the conference presentation, I watched a short scenario about a professor and their student, who needed to discuss their thesis. It went something like the following:

STUDENT: Hi Professor. I was hoping to talk to you about my thesis. I have a lot of questions.

PROFESSOR: *(not looking up)*: Oh, did we have an appointment?

STUDENT: No, but I thought, since it is your office hours …

PROFESSOR: *(starts packing up materials)*: Sorry, but I must get to a meeting that I just found out about. Drop me an email to schedule a time.

STUDENT: But you canceled the last time. Just a couple of quick questions, please.

PROFESSOR: Look, between classes and a publishing deadline, I am really busy. You're bright, I am sure you are doing better than you think. We'll talk about it soon. Email me.

STUDENT: I'm running out of time.

[The professor leaves. The student walks away dejected.]

The audience then held a discussion with the actors, who remained in character, about what they were thinking, feeling, and what they needed. The professor shared feeling overwhelmed and the pressure to publish to keep their job. The student shared feeling ignored and unimportant. This was in addition to being stressed and frustrated since they needed guidance on their thesis. Audience members then discussed in small groups ways the professor might better handle the situation. Following the small group audience discussions, the actors then performed the scenario again. This was the same scenario from the beginning, only this time audience members were allowed to stop the scenario if there was a problem to be addressed. Stopping the scenario gave an audience member the opportunity to enter the scenario as the professor and try an idea to improve the situation for the student. This was followed by the student giving feedback on how well the intervention worked, or did not work, for them. More than one audience member could volunteer to try an idea. Following each intervention, the professor reentered, and the scenario continued until an audience member again stopped the scenario to address a recognized challenge.

The interventions were small, often short, but usually changed the situation for the better. One person stopped the scenario, stepped in for the professor, and proceeded to give attention to the student, including making eye contact. After this brief intervention, the student shared how this simple action was reassuring. Another intervention was an audience member stepping in for the professor and explaining quickly to the student that they had to leave but took time to set up an appointment. The student's feedback included their preference that the professor not share so much of their stress, but they felt good about the appointment being set before leaving.

The workshop continued with other scenarios between the professor and the student. Once the first few audience volunteers intervened, several others participated at this level. Between the *Talkbacks* and *Interventions*, audience members gained many ideas to use in their own situations. This was true even for those who were not ready to join the scenario with an intervention.

Inspired by what I had witnessed and knowing its potential, I began investigating this type of theatre. My research not only included extensive reading about Augusto Boal and *Theatre of the Oppressed* but actually being imbedded in one of only two troupes I could find of this type in higher education. This resulted in my dissertation that would become a guide to developing my own troupe, *Giving Voice*, with our own style of interactive theatre based on *Theatre of the Oppressed*, which utilizes theatre for social change to bring diversity training experiences to a whole new level.

Background

The Giving *Voice Project* was developed in response to the findings of a 2009 Harvard study on issues of oppression called *Voices of Diversity: What Racial/Ethnic Minority Students Can Tell Us About Advantages and Disadvantages of Attending Predominantly White Colleges* (Caplan et al., 2009). The study, funded by the W.K. Kellogg Foundation, was conducted at four predominately white institutions (PWIs), including Missouri State University in the fall of 2008. The study showed all the universities could do better for their diverse students. Although the United States had just elected our first president of color, there appeared to be a type of backlash in the country. Comments ranged from denying President Obama was a United States citizen to the backhanded compliment that he had "gotten the Black vote because he was Black and gotten the white vote because he was light skinned and didn't sound like a Black person." A version of this popular sentiment made it into our first *Giving Voice* script. While some declared all our racial problems were over, this era seemed to compel us forward and backward at the same time. This was especially true on campuses of higher education, including ours.

The *Voices of Diversity* study found that several students of color had negative experiences with faculty, including a small portion who sensed a negative appraisal of their overall intelligence. Only a few believed that the university went out of its way to help a student who was doing poorly to stay in school. Other findings included feeling their racial/ethnic identity was not supported, feelings of not fitting in, and some students reported it had been suggested they had been admitted only because of affirmative action. Many respondents reported racial/ethnic microinsults and microinvalidations, as well as numerous forms of microaggressions presented in the guise of humor. These affronts came from faculty and staff, as well as other students.

These microaggressions take a toll on students. Many reported they do not believe that their ideas are respected by other undergraduates or teaching assistants/graduate students. During the time of the study, current students endure a variety of microaggressions, including from faculty and staff. These have been shared with *Giving Voice* troupe members for use in scenarios. Troupe members also report personal experiences of microaggressions. These have ranged from "jokes" about students of color being in college because of affirmative action to "compliments" about how well they speak. The frustration of not being accepted like others often leads to frustration and additional stress, especially when coming from friends. It certainly diminishes their higher education experience.

Microaggressions

"It's just a joke." These words are often used to cover everything from an unintended slight to a deeply cutting verbal assault. Microaggressions and/or macroaggressions are two of the main forms of insults that target a specific race, gender, sexual identity, disability, economic status, or overall difference of an individual.

Usually, microaggressions are used toward an individual, while macroaggressions are used toward everyone of a particular distinction. For instance, "You're so pretty for a black girl" or "You're really smart for a girl" are forms of microaggressions. These are also good examples of the challenge of objecting to, much less reporting, such behavior. Comments indicate that someone is pretty and smart. On the other hand, "Bisexuals just need to make up their mind" is directed at an entire group, in this case nullifying the existence of a whole group of people. A variety of policies and laws have been developed to protect targeted and/or marginalized groups from macroaggressions. Ironically, these suppressed macroaggressions have given rise to the more subtle microaggressions.

The larger, more obvious issues of oppression are rooted in many, much smaller slights, or what are called microaggressions. However, according to Sue et al. (2007), microaggressions are commonplace verbal, behavioral, or environmental indignities, whether intentional or unintentional, that communicate hostile, derogatory, or negative slights and insults to people on the basis of an aspect of the person's identity. In schools, it is simply referred to as bullying. They are usually subtle and mostly unintentional, unconscious, and possibly invisible to those not targeted. Therefore, they are difficult to confirm, due to plausible deniability or intent. Microaggressions are typically supported by everyday manifestations such as media images, literary characters, jokes, news reports, casual conversations, and institutional policies. In schools, social media is often the instrument of choice. They are often perpetrated by people who experience themselves as good, moral, and decent human beings who would never intentionally discriminate against others on the basis of race, gender, religion, or other differences.

Many bystanders of microaggressions, who do notice, often remain silent. There are a variety of excuses, such as educators talk of needing to cover curriculum, or like others, they are afraid they might make things worse. Sometimes, people are not sure how to handle the situation or are just caught so off guard they freeze. Unfortunately, silence indicates approval. No matter how well-intentioned, if a teacher does not address even the slightest microaggression against a student, they are telling that student they approve of whatever was said or done.

Impact of Microaggressions

Microaggressions are often the result of a veiled compliment, such as a white person telling a person of color that they are "articulate," or telling someone who is transgender that they don't "look" transgender. Microaggressions can worsen already difficult communications between persons of difference, which in turn increases subtle discrimination. By their smallness, they can seem too trivial to pursue action to be taken against the aggressor. They may be written off as too difficult to prove or too minor to report in a world where available redress may seem heavy-handed. According to *Lean In, Women in the Workplace*, while anyone can be on the receiving end of disrespectful behavior, microaggressions are more often directed at those with less power, such as women, people of color, and LGBTQ people (Women in the Workplace Study, 2022).

Consequently, people who are the target tend to try to "ignore" or "stuff them down" until the victim is with others who will "get it." If the victim has others available, they can process the event and its emotional toll. However, "pushing" these actions down emotionally, takes a toll, especially if you are alone in enduring these microaggressions. These subtle, commonplace indignities have harmful psychological impacts, including depression, low self-esteem, and trauma. Additionally, there is a higher suicide rate among the marginalized who endure microaggressions day after day. It is like constant dripping water that can wear away the toughest stone. Some have described living with constant microaggressions as "death by a thousand tiny cuts." However, once microaggressions are acknowledged then voice can be given to those suffering.

A New Style of Diversity Training

Due to my background in producing training videos and my passion for this type of work, I was approached for ideas to address some of the findings in order to improve our campus climate. It was suggested I develop a training video on diversity issues. Knowing the interactive limitations of film, I immediately thought of the research project I had just finished on the use of interactive theatre for professional development. While film can be informative, similar to live diversity training, it lacks the opportunity to practice what to do when you recognize the microaggression. Additionally, film does not evolve with each presentation, nor does it allow for any questions, clarifications, or discussions, much less interventions. I knew my own study, titled *The Use of Interactive Theatre as Professional Development in Higher Education to Reduce Alienation of Marginalized Groups*, would be a more effective approach. As a theatre artist and scholar, I knew the power of theatre. Brian Stokes Mitchell explained, "it has the power to transform an audience, an individual, or en masse, to transform them and give them an epiphanal experience that changes their life, opens their hearts and their minds and the way they think." I suggested developing our own interactive theatre troupe for professional development. Support came from the Provost and the Faculty Center for Teaching and Learning for the initial pilot project. Thus began the *Giving Voice* Project.

An engaging approach to improving cultural competence, theatre is used to directly address issues of oppression, including microaggressions. The *Giving Voice* Project was based on Augusto Boal's *Theater of the Oppressed*, a social-action theatre form building on Paulo Freire's *Pedagogy of the Oppressed*. The project was designed to portray the complexities and challenges of everyday situations. This is done through scenarios that shed light on discrimination; this discrimination, once named, can be combated. The forums provide a safe environment to confront our own biases and discuss their impact. A trained facilitator guides participants through a series of phases designed to help participants let go of reflexive thinking and acclimate to new paradigms in thinking. A typical training session is structured to build from fun, safe, and engaging games to challenging exercises that some participants may find uncomfortable as they face the realities and implications of stereotyping and their own privilege. Storytelling is the basis for theatre, thus, the voice of many is heard through the art of theatre.

Paulo Freire

Brazilian theorist Paulo Freire's pedagogy of learning evolved from the basis of theatre and was about the action of doing (Freire, 2005). Consequently, Freire viewed students as those oppressed by a hierarchical pedagogical process and suppressed by the educator in charge. In his book, *Pedagogy of the Oppressed* (2005), Freire contended action and reflection were essential components for developing true praxis. Dialogue was necessary for addressing a "world which is to be transformed and humanized" (p. 77). Freire further explained dialogue could not be from only one person delivering opinions, however learned, to others. Even a dialogue exchange for the knowledge of others is too simplistic and risks being an imposition of one truth.

Freire's approach to students being actively involved in their education by engaging with their teachers was the inspiration for Boal's development of *Theatre of the Oppressed.* Similar to Freire, Boal's approach to address oppression has been to actively engage the oppressed in their emancipation process. Theatrically, this stressed play-building and participatory performances rather than a one-sided presentation (Cohen-Cruz & Schutzman, 1994).

Augusto Boal

The *Giving Voice* Project was based on Augusto Boal's *Theatre of the Oppressed.* Originating in Brazil, Boal used theatre in streets, factories, legislatures, churches, and any place that needed light shed on issues and where people could participate in finding solutions to a variety of problems, including bullying, drugs, illiteracy, sexual abuse, gender, and racial discrimination, to name a few. This style of theatre went beyond presenting a problem in society. It went beyond discussions to reach a solution. It tested the solutions. The audience engaged in the scenario to see if a solution would work. They would not stop at one solution but would try numerous interventions to improve the situation. Most important, these interventions were tried in a safe place. Not every intervention works out well, especially not for everyone in the scenario. Sometimes they can even make the situation worse. But in a safe place, there are no repercussions, just knowledge about what not to do. This can be as important as the interventions that work out well.

These techniques, in some form or another, are now used worldwide to affect positive change. Boal developed this type of theatre to transform performance from its traditional delivery to a passive audience, a type of monologue, to a dialogue between the audience and the actors on stage. Boal experimented with many kinds of interactive theatre. His explorations were based on an understanding that dialogue is the common, healthy dynamic between all humans, all human beings desire and are capable of dialogue, and that when a dialogue becomes a monologue, oppression ensues (Babbage, 2004). Theatre is an extraordinary tool for transforming monologue into dialogue.

Boal also originated the concept of the *spect-actor*. Instead of an audience just being spectators, they were invited to join the scenario in order to improve the situation. Thus, the spectator becomes an actor or *spect-actor*. They take action. They become the protagonist of the scenario as a "rehearsal for reality" or as Boal described it, "rehearsal for life" (Cohen-Cruz & Schutzman, 2006). This became the goal for the *Giving Voice* Project, to get the audience involved or what is now referred to as *upstanders* rather than *bystanders*. Currently, the most common tactic used to handle oppression is to ignore it. It is easier to pretend to not hear a comment, not see a slight, or decide it is not your responsibility. However, silence indicates approval. Silence is complicity.

Most diversity training modules efficiently dispense relevant information. However, training is delivered to a largely passive audience without preparation or practice in using the information in actual, complex situations. While traditionally trained individuals are able to recognize oppression, they usually do not know what action to take or are afraid they will make things worse. *Giving Voice* forums provide a safe environment for audience members to step into the scenario and try their ideas to improve the situation. This is a powerful experience for the intervener and the audience that witnesses the action. Fortunately, in a safe space, interventions can be discovered to cause harm, and everyone learns what not to do. A young student teacher bravely volunteered to intervene and started by suggesting to make a chart of what would be attributed to Black students and what would be attributed to white students. Her idea was to narrow down topics for discussion in order to save arguments and find common ground. This idea was immediately met with negativity from the two Black characters. Even some audience members wanted to stop the intervention. Rather than accusing the student teacher of being racist, troupe members, in character, explained why that would be harmful to them. After this particular forum, I heard from several supervisors who shared that their own student teachers were grateful for this potentially harmful intervention. The reason they were grateful was because they thought the chart was a good idea.

Sometimes someone intervenes passionately by calling out the main oppressor, even berating them, sometimes aggressively, for their microaggression. This "victory" for the intervener soon takes a different turn during feedback. While the victim of the microaggression may have positive comments for someone standing up for them, some share stress of more attention drawn to them and being scared what the oppressor will do to them later. The oppressor reveals a much different reaction. They express feeling shut down and attacked. Often, explaining that they want to retaliate against the intervener or the victim later. *Giving Voice* works to call people "in" rather than "out" and hopes to instill this approach in the audience. In the spirit of Boal, who talked about the need to push society, since it does not move on its own, we work to push gently but firmly.

Systemic Oppression

The approach of *Giving Voice* is based on personal narratives; powerful true stories that reveal the heart of those who deal with some form of oppression, often on a daily basis. It is important to understand that oppression is systemic. It is the marginalizing and abuse of a group that, at least, is supported, and at worst, reinforced by society and institutions. These institutions include schools, churches, judicial, and government. Systems of oppression are historical and are intertwined in American culture, society, and even laws. These systems of oppression include racism, sexism, heterosexism, ableism, classism, ageism, and some religions. Whether the institution recognizes its part in reinforcing oppression, the result is an advantage for the dominant group. Oppression in one area bolsters oppression in other areas. While some oppressions are easily recognized, many are hidden in plain sight due to being systemic.

During a *Giving Voice* forum, an audience member was asking about the backgrounds of the characters. At one point, they asked someone if they were from a *normal* family. This started a whole new dialogue instigated by a character with two dads and another character who lived with their grandmother. Systems of oppression are individual, institutional, and societal, and their effects on people have a long history deeply rooted in American culture (National Museum of African American History & Culture, 2023).

> Whether we are aware of it or not, we are all assigned multiple social identities. Within each category, there is a hierarchy - a social status with dominant and non-dominant groups. As with race, dominant members can bestow benefits to members they deem "normal," or limit opportunities to members that fall into "other" categories. A person of the non-dominant group can experience oppression in the form of limitations, disadvantages, or disapproval. They may even suffer abuse from individuals, institutions, or cultural practices. "Oppression" refers to a combination of prejudice and institutional power that creates a system that regularly and severely discriminates against some groups and benefits other groups.
>
> (National Museum of African American History & Culture, 2023)

Social activist, Audre Lorde, contends "there is no hierarchy of oppressions." Therefore, we must fight against all oppression, all at once. Lorde further recognized that, "although we possess different identities, we are all connected as human beings" (National Museum of African American History & Culture, 2023).

The impact of systemic oppression is felt on a personal level. Therefore, *Giving Voice* uses an interpersonal approach in the way the audience interacts with the characters in a forum. Connection on an interpersonal level is key to the success of *Giving Voice*. Our shared humanity is what makes understanding possible.

Why Giving Voice

Although, for simplicity, I will explain the process of developing a troupe using college students as a reference, these techniques can be applied to any group, any age, in any organization, who wish to make a positive change in this world, especially in their own environment. The topics explored by a troupe are determined by what issues need to be addressed in a particular environment. These issues can range from racial and LGBTQ+ oppression to sexual harassment. The key is to know what your situation needs. Almost always, there is an oppressor and an oppressed. Although these are strong words, they are the simplest to describe the situation when someone feels they cannot speak up for themselves or they are not being heard.

The Evolution of Giving Voice

Giving Voice embodies the essence of the Missouri State University Public Affairs Mission as it promotes ethical leadership, cultural competence, and community engagement. In the ten years since the *Giving Voice* Project resulted in the first forum for the leadership team of the university, *Giving Voice* has held over 270 forums and reached over 11,000 participants. These forums have been held nationwide, for public schools, other colleges and universities to community organizations, medical facilities, national conferences, and international businesses.

Often groups want more forums to reach others in their organizations. However, having *Giving Voice* return as often as needed is not feasible. Some groups lament they do not have their own troupe. Yet having an in-house troupe is the most effective plan. For instance, schools know what the challenges are and the types of bullying that are happening in classrooms, halls, and on buses. Moreover, the students know, and they are the ones that will make up the troupe.

Reading the resources available and participating in training workshops for developing a troupe and facilitating forums is also not often feasible. Therefore, the following is a direct, simplified guide to this important work. While there are several recommended books and a few workshops, this guide can serve as easy access to development and facilitating a troupe to improve your own environment. While this is written for educational settings, there will be examples of how it can be used in the workplace and other organizations in Chapter 12. Everyone deserves a safe environment, in which to thrive.

> Theatre is a form of knowledge: it should and can also be a means of transforming society. Theatre can help us build our future, rather than just waiting for it.
>
> (Augusto Boal)

References

Babbage, F. (2004). *Augusto Boal*. New York: Routledge.

Caplan, P., Nettles, M., Millett, C., Miller, S., DiCrecchio, N., & Chu, T. (2009). The Voices of Diversity: What Racial/Ethnic Minority Students Can Tell Us About Advantages and Disadvantages of Attending Predominantly White Colleges. *Preliminary Report for Missouri State University*. 1–74.

Cohen-Cruz, J., & Schutzman, M. (Eds.). (1994). *Playing Boal: Theatre, therapy, activism*. London: Routledge.

Cohen-Cruz, J., & Schutzman, M. (Eds.). (2006). *A Boal companion: Dialogues on theatre and cultural politics*. New York: Routledge.

Freire, P. (2005). *Pedagogy of the oppressed*. New York: The Continuum International.

Mitchell, B. (2024, May 6). *What is Brechtian Theatre?* The Superprof Blog. Retrieved May 14, 2024, from https://www.superprof.co.uk/blog/the-brechtian-method-and-epic-theatre/

National Museum of African American History & Culture. (2023, August 24). *Social Identities and Systems of Oppression*. https://nmaahc.si.edu/learn/talking-about-race/topics/social-identities-and-systems-oppression

Sue, D., Capodilupo, C., Torino, G., Bucceri, J., Holder, A., Nadal, K., & Esquilin, M. (2007). Racial microaggressions in everyday life: Implications for clinical practice. *American Psychologist*, *62*(4), 271–286.

Women in the Workplace Study. (2022, October 18). Lean In. https://leanin.org/women-in-the-workplace

2 Choosing the Troupe

Call for Troupe Members

> When I started kindergarten, I had lots of friends. Then one day everyone stopped talking to me and no one would play with me. Finally, I asked my former best friend why? She said it was because I killed Jesus (auditioner for *Giving Voice*).

This story was shared by a Jewish student during a *Giving Voice* audition. This hurt from kindergarten was still as deep, if not deeper for this college student. The work done by *Giving Voice* is best served by *those* that know oppression, *those* that know words hurt, and *those* that know the pain of others' silence while they endure the hurt. However, as much as a troupe needs people that understand being the target of oppression, there is a need for those that have more privilege. While white males are not the only ones, they are the predominant oppressors. A troupe needs people of privilege to use their stature to help tell the stories of the oppressed. They must be able to say offensive things in a scenario so another can give voice to the effect it has on them. A troupe might incorporate the opening story in a scenario by having someone "joke" about Jews killing Jesus. This allows the Jewish student to explain how scary that kind of talk is. It is not only hurtful, but that "joke" led to the murder of millions of Jews and is used today to attack Jewish people. When a troupe member says something awful, they must believe it is for the greater good.

Passion for the Work

Troupe members should be more interested in addressing issues of oppression than learning acting techniques. This is especially true since this type of theatre does not require trained actors. One of the recommended books is *Games for Actors and Non-Actors* (Boal, 1992). As long as someone has a passion to help and can talk in front of others, then they can be a part of the troupe.

DOI: 10.4324/9781032676883-2

Willingness to Serve as Representatives

The issues you want to address will determine the troupe members needed. For instance, if you need to address racial issues then you will need members who are racially diverse. The same is true for members of the LGBTQ+ community, as well as gender, abilities, and socio-economic issues. Often, troupe members will relate to issues, having lived through many of the situations to be depicted. It is important for someone that can relate to play the characters being oppressed. Having white characters talk about people of color who are their friends and what their friends have been through is not the same. The Black friend needs to talk about how scared he was when the police pulled over his car leaving Taco Bell. The white friend can talk about the police asking her if she was okay.

The Need for Oppressors and Victims

Of course, to address the issues, there must be characters that say something that needs to be addressed. Such as, a white male will likely be asked to portray an oppressor at times. A person of color will need to portray a character who does not speak up for themselves but will get the opportunity to share why that is and how hurtful words can be. Often, troupe members are the ones who will speak up for themselves but need to portray those that cannot.

Advertising for Auditioners

Therefore, auditioners must be able to say and do things in character they, personally, would not say or do. The troupe members that are asked to portray someone oppressive need to understand it is needed to bring this behavior to light and allow the voices of those affected to be heard. It is a rewarding but challenging commitment. Advertise for troupe members from all areas, explaining what the work entails, including the time commitment, and the chance to make a positive difference. Advertisements should encourage non-theatre students to audition. In the spirit of Boal, invite auditioners to help push society to do better.

Willingness to Meet Individuals Where They Are

Explain the unique opportunity to participate in interactive theatre and be a part of the solution to address issues of oppression or bullying. Auditioners do not have to be trained actors. They will receive the training they need for this type of work. They will learn about a different kind of theatre, improvisation, and research for and development of scripts. Auditioners should be made aware they must be able to say and do things in character that they would not personally do or say. This should be in the advertisement, the application form, and reiterated during the auditions. There are a lot of possible social media avenues for advertising in addition to posters (see Appendix A and B for example posters).

Calling People in Rather Than Calling People Out

> *That was a terrible audience. Can you believe the things they were saying? "Why can't I use normal pronouns rather than 'they' and 'them' when I address a student?*
> *It's proper grammar."*
> — a *Giving Voice* troupe member's reaction after a forum

Giving Voice holds forums for all kinds of audiences. Sometimes, it is for groups that recognize most of the microaggressions that are portrayed. They often have interventions to improve the situation depicted in the scenario that are effective and positive. Then, there are the audience with members who ask questions about pronouns, such as the one above. They may question what is wrong with the confederate flag or try to explain that all lives matter. I remind the troupe, that these are the audiences we want to reach. It is why we do the work. These audience members are not "terrible," and often a calm discussion with the characters, sometimes with the actors after a forum, reveals sincere people with good hearts who have not heard a different perspective. Often, faculty and staff want to do what is best for students and be allowed to learn about issues without being called out and judged. Once, after a forum for bus drivers, a no-nonsense gentleman continued to explain to some of the troupe members that he wanted to do the right thing, but he didn't see the need to change. He was 60 years old, and it was too hard, especially with students changing names and pronouns. The troupe members listened respectfully, and then one shared the importance of being seen for who they were. They explained the mental and emotional anguish of not being accepted was, at times, overwhelming. They also explained their old name was considered their dead name. The respect shown by using their chosen name and pronouns not only made them feel seen but also whole and accepted. The man asked what to do because he forgets and does it wrong. He was assured a quick apology or acknowledgment was all that was needed. He was then encouraged to keep trying because it could make a positive difference in a student's life.

Holding Auditions

Pre-Audition

If possible, skip the traditional, initial round of auditions and have those interested come for one unique audition. These pre-auditions should only be used to determine callbacks for the main audition if there is an abundance of interest.

This pre-audition should be as low risk as possible to encourage all interested. This could be a prepared, very short, monologue or audition in groups to participate in a few Boal exercises and some discussions. This will give the facilitator a chance to get to know the auditioners a little better, see if they are willing to do some of the basic Boal exercises, are supportive of others, and then decide who to have come to the main auditions. If you do not anticipate an abundance of auditioners, have anyone interested sign up for a main audition time slot. These are extended time slots of 45 to 75 minutes depending on the number of auditioners in a group to work together, usually not more than ten.

Representation Matters

Part of what you will be looking for are students who can cover a diversity of characters, such as racially diverse, LGBTQ+, or religious. One of the ironies of this work is essentially using one character to speak for a group of people, even though that character makes a point of often being asked to speak for an entire group, such as one person of color does not speak for all people of color. The same is true for all the characters; however, there are common oppressions that can be addressed, such as constantly being asked to represent an entire group, being followed in stores, or having people touch their hair.

Willingness and Ability to Share

For the main audition, the actors are asked to be prepared to share a true story of oppression. Be sure to give a time limit of one to two minutes, as these can sometimes take up too much of the audition time. The story should be about a time they experienced some form of discrimination, bullying, sexual harassment, or other type of oppression due to race, gender, religion, sexual orientation, etc. This story can either be their own true story, someone else's story, or it can be fictionalized; however, if they choose to tell a story not their own, they must tell it as if it were true and happened to them. After all, this is what they will be doing, sharing others' and sometimes their own stories. If someone does not feel like they have been oppressed, they can talk about what they have seen or explain why they want to be a part of the troupe. The main audition space should be established as a safe zone for the various stories to be shared and readings from already scripted scenarios. Basically, what happens in *Giving Voice* stays in *Giving Voice*. Even temporary auditioners must agree that stories shared, and improvisation of oppression do not leave the group, and there is no judgment. This is also a key understanding of the troupe.

Sharing Circle

Have each group in the main audition sit in a semi-circle so everyone can be seen. Assure them they are in a safe space and what is said stays there. Begin with each auditioner sharing their name and in what ways they are diverse.

Remind them of diversity that is beyond what people can see or think they see. Such sharing can include diversity such as racial, sexuality, gender, religion, and abilities. There should also be a place to share these on the audition form (see Appendix C). This is your initial impression, but remain open to possibilities. You will have a first impression vocally and physically, but also an insight as to how the auditioner sees themself, especially when it comes to diversity.

Sharing the Personal, Sharing Your Why

Next in the auditions is to have each one share their true story of oppression in less than two minutes, but allow more time if needed. Remember this can be something that has actually happened to them, or they tell someone else's story as if it did happen to them. Be aware that this could be emotional for some, depending on their story. This is when it may be necessary to not adhere to the time set. Be prepared to give the support needed. Always acknowledge and honor each auditioner for trusting to share.

You will learn a great deal from this important exercise beyond if the auditioners are prepared with a story. You will gain valuable knowledge about the students, what they have been through and how they handle whatever happened to them. Sometimes, they will share someone else's story, which can also be informative. This may reveal a true understanding, especially of white students who recognize their privilege. It can also demonstrate they are ready to do the work of giving voice to others. There are also insights to be gained about the other auditioners from how they handle these stories and support each other.

Cold Readings and Improvisation

Finally, have the auditioners do cold readings using a page or two from either a script included in this book or one you have developed from a past troupe. If possible, have each auditioner read for more than one role. If time permits, give them the option to read a role they have not read but wish to try or read the same role again. Try to make sure each auditioner feels they have done their best. At the end of each reading, try some improv similar to the *Talkback* Phase of a forum. This could be possible questions from the audience, such as "Why did you get upset when you saw a group of Muslims outside the student union?" or "Why is it important for you to let people know you are biracial?" This lets you know if they can come up with an appropriate answer for their character. Do not worry if it is not what you expect. Remember they are reacting for the first time to this character. Also, watch for interactions among the characters during the cold readings. Are they able to converse in character and make a point with the other characters?

Cold readings and improvisation can be challenging for even trained actors. Make sure you are looking at the full picture when considering someone. Even though they might not seem ready to perform with a forum already, look for potential. Strongly consider their sincerity, support of others auditioning with them, and their passion to make a difference.

Casting and Troupe Size Considerations

How Many?

The number of actors needed will vary depending on the situation and how easily available the members are for forums. This is a strong consideration for students who might need to miss classes for forums. Although the number needed varies depending on the scenario developed, four to six troupe members is a good start. Ideally, there would be 8–12, in order to cover characters without using the same person constantly. Eighteen is the maximum recommended, and that is during the building phase. Once a troupe is established, members will leave for various reasons, particularly students who graduate. New members of the troupe will be going through training and ensemble building with the established troupe, thus the larger number of members up to 18.

Small Troupe Advantage

The smaller troupe has the advantage of getting to know one another easier than the larger troupe. This makes building the important ensemble easier also. As they get to know each other personally and in their respective characters, they are able to anticipate and react better in forums. They also can tell if something has been said or happened in a forum that has upset the actor, rather than or in addition to the character. This is an essential aspect of successful forums and emotionally healthy troupe members. Troupe members meet before forums to get focused and review possible challenges. More importantly, troupe members should check in with each other after a forum. You never know if something triggered a member. You should also check on the cast after a forum.

Large Troupe Advantage

Larger troupes have the advantage of sharing the forums and sometimes the characters. This gives members a break from forums or a break from always playing the same part. This is especially needed for those that play the main oppressor. As for rehearsals and building the ensemble, the larger troupe will come from casting new members before you lose current members. By this time the current troupe has grown close, but they know the importance of making the new members feel a part of the ensemble. A large number of troupe members can be challenging, especially making sure everyone feels included and balancing the casting for forums. A large enough space for training exercises might also be a consideration. However, it is rewarding to see the current troupe's leadership and caring for the new members. This is what makes the larger number possible and worthwhile.

What is the Need?

What voices need to be heard? Casting, of course, is based mostly on need, which in turn is based on the stories that need to be told and what is being said and done to people that can be depicted by members of the troupe. In predominately white southwest Missouri, there was plenty of oppression toward race, gender, and the LGBTQ+ community. Sometimes, the challenge is to find representation willing to join the troupe. It is okay to advertise and recruit from specific sources, such as organizations.

How to Find Diverse Auditioners

The best recruitment has been holding forums for the groups that need to be heard. Often, audience members will ask about joining the troupe. Ideally, the characters need to be played by someone from that group, such as bi-racial, LGBTQ+, abilities, and certain religions. Although characters can take many forms and intersectionality, begin with characters for the stories that need to be told. The troupe can always expand to other scripts if needed. In addition to members representing a particularly oppressed group, there is a need for the oppressor. While particular troupe members are necessary, sometimes auditioners need the troupe. There is a growth and often a transformation that comes from doing this type of work. Once the cast is in place, it is time for training and to learn interview and research skills. Most importantly, the ensemble building begins.

Reference

Boal, A. (1992). *Games for actors and non-actors* (A. Jackson, Trans.). Routledge.

Appendix A

Society does not move on its own; it has to be pushed
– Augusto Boal

Want to Help Push?

Giving voice

Auditions

(Day, Date), Audition Options Starting at (Time)

or by special arrangement

Troupe Members Needed for (YEAR)

All Majors Are Encouraged to Audition

Giving Voice is looking for new troupe members representing our wonderfully diverse world through race, gender, sexuality, religion, etc., to join us for the (NEXT YEAR)

For more information or to sign up for one of the groups audition times scan the QR code below:

If you have questions or need to audition at a different time – Contact (NAME) at (EMAIL ADDRESS) (Subject: Giving Voice Auditions)

Theatre is a form of knowledge: it should and can also be a means of transforming society. Theatre can help us build our future, rather than just waiting for it.
– Augusto Boal, Director and Educationalist-Theatre of the Oppressed

Appendix B

Want to Make a Difference? Be a Part of the Solution

Giving Voice

Auditions

(Day, Date), Audition Options Starting at (Time)

or by special arrangement

Troupe Members Needed for (YEAR)

Non-Theatre Majors Are Encouraged to Audition

Giving Voice is looking for new troupe members to join us for the (NEXT YEAR). This is a unique opportunity to participate in Interactive Theatre for Social Justice, based on Augusto Boal's *Theatre of the Oppressed*, and to be a part of the solution to address issues of oppression happening here and beyond. The basic rehearsal schedule will also be used to learn about *Theatre of the Oppressed*, improvisation, and research for and development of script(s). You will also learn how to workshop a script and develop appropriate in-depth characters. We will have other meeting times for performances, but this will be coordinated with the troupe members.

This is a rewarding but challenging commitment. You must be able to say and do things in character that you personally would not say or do. As a troupe member you may be asked to portray someone oppressive in order to bring this behavior to light and allow the voices of those affected to be heard. As Augusto Boal says, "Society does not move on its own; it has to be pushed."

If you wish to be considered for the troupe to help "push," contact (NAME) at (EMAIL ADDRESS) (Subject: Giving Voice Auditions) to sign up for the **1st audition group-3:30 to 4:45** or the **2nd group-4:45 to 6:00** or work out another time, if possible.

Please prepare a story (1, no more than 2, minutes in length) about a time you experienced some form of discrimination, bullying, sexual harassment, or other type of oppression due to race, gender, religion, sexual orientation, etc. This story can either be your own true story, someone else's story, or it can be fictionalized; however, if you choose to tell a story not your own, you must tell it as if it were true and happened to you. You will also be asked to read an existing scenario and possibly improvise an intervention through the use of the scenario with others auditioning and/or current troupe members. Groups will be auditioned together in the 75-minute time slots. Plan to be there the whole time.

To sign up for an audition or if you have questions – Contact (NAME) at (EMAIL ADDRESS) (Subject: Giving Voice Auditions)

Theatre is a form of knowledge: it should and can also be a means of transforming society. Theatre can help us build our future, rather than just waiting for it.

– Augusto Boal, Director and Educationalist-Theatre of the Oppressed

Appendix C

Giving Voice Auditions: (DATE), (PLACE). Time Slots Are Available Beginning at (TIME) or by Special Arrangement

Also, email if you have any questions.

Email:

1. Name

2. Please select **ALL** time slots you are available to audition on (DAY), (DATE).

   Check all that apply.

   - [ ] 3:30–4:15
   - [ ] 4:20–5:05
   - [ ] 5:10–5:55
   - [ ] I cannot be available at any of those times. I will email to arrange a different time.

3. Email

4. Pronouns

5. Phone Number:

6. Degree and Major (example: BS in Physics):

7. Class Status:

Mark only one oval.

- Freshperson
- Sophomore
- Junior
- Senior
- Graduate Student

8. Expected graduation date

9. GPA:

10. What are the ways in which you are diverse, such as race, sexual orientation, gender, religion, etc. (be specific with what you are willing to share)

11. What discrimination or oppression, such as ethnicity, religion, gender, sexual orientation, gender identity, etc., can you personally relate to or have intimate knowledge of through friends or family? (list all that apply you are willing to share)

12. Are you willing to portray a character that is not who you are personally or believe in, such as racist, sexist, homophobic, anti-religious, rapist, etc.? (Our work must have those characters in order to get the voices out for those that are being oppressed.)

Mark only one oval.

- YES
- NO
- MAYBE

13. Are you willing to participate in the Title IX forums on sexual harassment, assault, etc. (information only, your answer will not affect casting)

Mark only one oval.

- YES
- NO
- MAYBE

14. Why do you want to join Giving Voice? (1–3 sentences)

3 Training the Ensemble

Troupe Safe Zone for Ensemble

"I love the acceptance I feel in Giving Voice. No matter what has happened, when I go to *Giving Voice* rehearsal, there is a calmness that seems to help me breathe" (*Giving Voice* troupe member). The importance of building not only an ensemble but also a *Theatre of the Oppressed* style ensemble is the key to the success of the *Giving Voice* troupe. Have your troupe think of themselves as an acting company, with the responsibilities and commitment that are expected of any cast of a show. Establishing a safe environment is the priority of the first rehearsal with new troupe members. The goal is a safe place physically, mentally, and emotionally. Start with typical exercises for a theatre cast. These include physical warmups and games, usually silly games that let the troupe members relax and have fun while they get comfortable with each other. This comfort level includes physical contact for many of the exercises and games.

First Rehearsal Exercises

At the first gathering have the members circle up and explain the importance of a safe place for all members with no judgment. Now is a good time to check in with the members about physical contact, since several exercises require contact. Start with the basics, such as names, their year in school, major and one other piece of background they are comfortable to share. Even if all the members know each other, they may be surprised by what they learn. Then, start with some basic warmups for a cast. Then get them on their feet!

Contact

Instruct everyone to make physical contact with everyone else and give them a smile. This, of course, does not apply to anyone requesting to not have physical contact made with them. The physical contact can be anything they are comfortable with using, such as a handshake, touching elbows, fist bumps, etc. Eventually, many will be sharing hugs.

DOI: 10.4324/9781032676883-3

Circle Up

Standing in a circle, start with a simple, fun exercises such as the following:

Magnetic Smile

Without words or large physical gestures, each member is to get a smile from each of the other members. Once they have received a smile they are to sit down in their place. To do that they need to get each person to look at them and give them a smile as they receive a smile. This is not a contest to see who can keep from smiling. This is a terrific beginning exercise of giving support to each other and making sure each person gets what they need. They do get to tell anyone who sits down who does not get a smile from them.

Neutral Position

Have everyone stand back up in the circle and freeze. Have each one look around at the wonderful diversity that is their troupe, even from the physicality in the way they stand and hold themselves. Then have them relax. This is a basic actor exercise of awareness of different physical choices that are possible for a character. From this have them go to a neutral stance with feet shoulder width apart and close, if not, parallel, knees relaxed, arms relaxed by sides, and head up with neck relaxed.

The Drop

Starting a neutral position, talk to the actors through relaxing their head forward, followed by their shoulders, their arms and their back as they start to bend forward with the arms relaxed, bending all the way to touch the ground or as close as they can. Their head and arms should be relaxed to the point if you come by and touch their head or arms, they swing freely. If they do not, remind them that they need to relax. The dropped-down position is held for a count of 20. They should then take a deep breath and, on the exhale, try to stretch a little bit further. Hold for another count of 20. Take a deep breath, and on the exhale, try to bend just a little bit further. After another count of 20, they should start to roll back up into a standing position trying to keep everything relaxed until standing. They can imagine they are stacking their vertebrae one on top of the other. A good addition to this exercise is to have them continue the roll-up by lifting their arms to the ceiling and on their tiptoes stretching as high as they can. Most will feel a natural impulse to yawn. Encourage that impulse with the addition to vocalize it. Vocalizing a yawn is one of the best voice warmups. Overall, *The Drop* with the vocalized yawn is one of the best single exercises for warming up and energizing the body and voice.

Contact Warmups

There are a variety of leg and arm warmups that require a partner. Using these partner warmups has an additional important component beyond just a physical warmup. This is another way for your troupe to get to know and become comfortable with each other as you build the ensemble. Always have them switch partners for each stretch. If you are integrating new members into the cast this is a good opportunity to mix new members with current members by partnering them together. You also want to consciously partner actors who will play against each other such as the oppressor and the oppressed. The more your troupe members get to know each other the easier they can accept what they will hear from each other during forums. This will also be true for rehearsal improvisations. How many of these exercises you do during the first rehearsal depends on how much time you have.

Unique

Tell the troupe members to think of something unique about themselves that they think will not be like anyone else. This can be an experience, travel, celebrity meeting, physical trait, etc. Next, they are to meet one-on-one with each of the other members and both share that unique aspect about themselves. They continue to have these conversations until they have shared with everyone. Then have them circle up and indicate a member, ask the group what is unique about them. Continue until each person has been acknowledged. This is a great icebreaker and ensemble builder.

Boal Games, Exercises, Training, and Other Ensemble Builders

It is best to introduce the first Boal type exercise or game during the first rehearsal. Each of the following games serves several purposes. First and foremost, they build the ensemble through the fun, challenges, and discussions that come from participating in and examining what they do and feel. Even the games that most challenge how they see the world and themselves usually start with a low-risk or fun component. Reassure troupe members they may decline to participate or step away from any game. No judgment. They should always protect themselves.

After each game, have the troupe members circle up to *Debrief* the game. The debrief is important for the members to reflect and process what they have experienced. This is essential to gaining the most from their experiences. It is also a good time to check in on how they have been affected. Most debriefs can start with questioning how it went or their initial reaction. Always ask for input on how the game can be applied to the work of the troupe.

Guide them, if necessary, but as much as possible, let the troupe members share rather than you tell them what impressions they should have from the exercise. If you feel they have missed something, you can always ask after everyone has had a chance to share. However, it is good to summarize what they have shared and are taking away from each exercise or game.

Build Leadership

Use the book, *Games for Actors and Non-Actors* by Augusto Boal (1992), to share with a troupe member between rehearsals. Ask for a volunteer to take the book with them and find an exercise they think would be good for the group. They are to be prepared to lead the exercise during the next rehearsal. They should also lead the *Debrief.*

Begin Script Development

There are many components to developing the script, and ideas can come from several areas. *Check ins* with your troupe not only give them a chance to share their personal status but can often be something that happened to them that might be developed as part of a script. *Check ins* should also include positive sharing, even if you need to ask specifically for this. Another source of script material should come from the troupe members as researchers interviewing others. The other main source will come from the headlines. Script development will be explained in detail in the next chapter.

Subsequent Rehearsals

In addition to the usual ensemble-building exercises for a regular theatre cast, the troupe needs to face their own biases and develop the trust needed to improvise the stories they bring to rehearsal. Games are fundamental to *Theatre of the Oppressed* and this type of theatre. They allow participants, both actors and non-actors, to expand their imaginations and recognize then deconstruct vernacular language and habitual behaviors, while questioning previously unrecognized societal structures of power and oppression. Skillfully facilitated, these games also build that essential safe and trusting ensemble. Of course, the fact that many of them are fun is an added bonus.

Games for Actors and Non-Actors by Augusto Boal has an abundance of these games and exercises. The games the troupe engages in for training range from simplistic to multi-layered, but all are thought-provoking.

Establish Ground Rules

Essential to the development of the troupe and a safe environment is the creation of ground rules. These rules should be established early by the troupe members and include a safety word (i.e., mercy, aspirin, persnickety, etc.). There is a potential during the improvisation of a scenario, when an actor's character says something that penetrates to another actor's own feelings and experiences in a way that is hurtful. The safe word is used to stop the improv and support the actor. This safe word is available for use any time, for any reason, especially during forums. Examples of rules include:

Assume the best of each other
Use "I" statements
Acknowledge feelings
Speak up if you do not feel safe or something bothers you
Be sensitive of others
Challenge self to deal with difficult issues
Leave time to debrief or process

The last rule listed is crucial for the games and exercises to be meaningful. Each game should be followed by a debriefing session. Processing what happened during games or exercises helps troupe members to recognize and confront issues such as biases, privilege, power, and oppression. This also helps to ensure the actors are emotionally well before leaving rehearsal.

Other Considerations

- Establish an expectation for the beginning of rehearsals. Contact is a great requirement to start the rehearsal, followed by circling up for exercises. Be sure to allow anyone to opt out of contact. There must be consent. During the first few rehearsals, have them do the Drop and other exercises that you feel are beneficial. Eventually you can move away from the physical warmups as they become more comfortable with each other and have established the routine of gathering together in a circle.
- Have the volunteer who took home the *Games for Actors and Non-Actors* book take over leadership. They should lead their chosen exercise, including the *Debrief.*
- Continue with one or two of the following Boal exercises, depending on the time you have. The order can be changed, but do leave the higher risk exercises until last. This should give the troupe time to establish trust with each other and with you.
- Work on scripts and character development, including *Backstories* and *Talking Points*, and rehearse.

The different games used to train the troupe help build that important ensemble, but they also help troupe members let go of reflexive thinking and acclimate to new paradigms in thinking.

Recommended Games and the Order to Be Used for Training

Walk-Stop

> *I think of Giving Voice as a family. One where I can be myself, seen, and accepted.*
>
> —*Giving Voice* troupe member

Objective: Introduce troupe members to a fun exercise that will start to build an ensemble and get them thinking beyond their current conceptions.
When to use: Early in the ensemble building-even first
Procedure:

- Everybody gets into pairs.
- Begin by having the troupe members walk around the space. Instruct them that when you say, "walk," they walk and when you say, "stop," they stop.
  Do this for less than a minute. Have them stop and brag on how well they follow directions. ☺
  Explain they are ready to change things up.
- **Walk/Stop** reverse: Now when you say, "stop," they walk and when you say, "walk," they stop. Give these directions, stopping and starting them several times. Try to see if you can get some to walk when you say "walk" and stop when you say "stop" for a short time. This works well after talking to them about how well they are doing.
  (Now add another layer)
- **Name/Clap** reverse: Instruct them when you say, "name," they clap and if you say, "clap," they say their name. This is in addition to the current "stop" they walk and "walk" they stop.
  Randomly call out these four directions, trying to catch them doing the original meaning for the word rather than the new meaning. Comment they are doing so well that you are confident they can handle something more complicated such as another possible layer:
- **Jump/Dance** reverse: Instruct them when you say, "jump," they dance and if you say, "dance," they jump. This is in addition to the other two sets of reversed directions.
  Do all these for a short time. Finally, have them stop by saying "walk" and possibly end by saying a fast sequence of these new directions, such as "Jump, Name, Stop."
  If you want yet another layer, use the following, but the first three are usually enough to get them to recognize the challenges.
- **Knees/Arms** reverse: If you say, "knees," they put their arms in the air (then continue) and if you say, "arms," they put their hands on their knees (take 3 steps then continue).

Debriefing Walk/Stop Topics

- Initial thoughts about what they just experienced
- Fun watching each other and themselves not get it right
- Frustration, especially as more layers were added
- Realizing how easily they follow what others do, even though sometimes it is wrong
- Difficulty of new rules that are different from what they know so well
- How does this relate to people from another culture or speaking a different language?
- Relation to the troupe's work.

Person to Person

> *Some things weren't appropriate, depending on who my partner was.*
>
> —*Giving Voice* troupe member

Objective: Troupe members should become more comfortable with each other.

When to use: Early in the ensemble building, after knowing if everyone is comfortable with contact. Be prepared to make modifications for those not comfortable with contact, including allowing them to not participate or eventually lead.

Procedure:

- Everybody gets into pairs.
- The leader calls out the names of parts of the body, which the partners must join together; for instance, "Head-to-head." The partners must join their heads together; or "Foot to elbow" – one partner's foot must touch the other's elbow (and vice versa, at the same time, if it is possible).
- Continue to call out parts of the body. The game is cumulative, i.e., when the partners have conjoined two parts of their bodies they must keep those together while carrying out the next instruction. The actors can make the contacts in any way they choose, sitting, standing, lying, etc.
- After four or five instructions that have tangled the pairs together and taken the game to the limit of physical possibility, the leader shouts "Person to person!"
- The pairs separate and everyone finds a different partner – then the process starts again.
- Troupe members can take turns being the ones to call the instructions, again, building that leadership and confidence of each member with the others.

Debriefing Person-to-Person Topics

- Initial thoughts about what they just experienced
- Fun or frustration trying to manage, especially as more connections were asked

- Power dynamics between partners (size, gender, social norms, etc.)
- Sharing power
- Relation to the troupe's work

Columbian Hypnosis

> *I felt so powerful when I was the leader. Then I had to follow someone and lead another person. Leading was not my first priority, so they had some hard movements to do.*
>
> —*Giving Voice* troupe member

The name Columbian Hypnosis comes from Boal's work to develop wordless techniques with indigenous Latin Americans, specifically Columbians.

Objective: Realize the lack of communication and empathy for others when in power or looking out for themselves.

When to use: Early in the ensemble building, as this is a low-risk game with profound results.

Procedure:

- Divide the group into pairs, especially members who do not know each other well.
- The partners need to decide who is A and who is B.
- Explain that A will "hypnotize" B with their hand and B must keep their face just a few inches from A's hand at all times, trying to keep that distance throughout the exercise Instruct A to guide B into all sorts of positions, using forgotten muscles, in order to use their body in a different way.
- After a short time, A and B should change responsibilities and B leads A.
- There are variations such as dividing the group into 3s. A "hypnotizes" B with one hand and C using their other hand. They may do entirely different movements at any time.
- Experiment with larger groups with more than one doing the "hypnosis," such as A guides B and C plus C guides D.

Debriefing Columbian Hypnosis Topics

- Initial thoughts about what they just experienced
- Power dynamics
- Following mindlessly
- Forgetting about the one you are guiding because you are concentrating on yourself
- Relation to the troupe's work

One Person We Fear, One Person is Our Protector

> *It was hard to protect myself and someone else. Honestly, I forgot I was someone's protector. You never know who you might be able to help if you thought about others rather than yourself.*
>
> —*Giving Voice* troupe member

Objective: Know the feeling of being protected and, at the same time, protecting someone else.

When to use: After the troupe has played some low-risk games and is starting to build the trust needed for an ensemble.

Procedure:

- Spread the group out around the room. This is a silent game.
- Instruct each of them to choose one other person in the room who, for the purposes of this game only, they fear. They should do this without saying or indicating anything.
- Once everyone has made their choice, have them move around the room trying to keep as far away from the person they have chosen to fear. They should do so without letting that person become aware of the fact that they have chosen them as the one they fear.
- After a short time ask them to stop moving.
- Now ask everyone to think of another person to be their protector. Again, their choice should not be able to tell that they have been chosen as such.
- Now, their goal is to keep their protector between themself and the person they fear. Again, this should be done without letting the others know they are their protector or the one they fear.
- After a short time, count down from 10 to 1 as the person feared is going to "attack." After you say the number "one," have everyone freeze in place.
- They should look around for a moment to see where everyone ended up. Then relax but still in place.
- Ask members of the group to acknowledge who they feared and who was their protector. Did they manage to keep their protector between themselves and the one they feared?

Debriefing One Person We Fear, One Person Is Our Protector Topics

- Initial thoughts about what they just experienced
- Forgetting they were someone's protector and were only thinking of themselves
- Discovering they were someone's protector only to realize that they were the one that person feared
- Relation to the troupe's work

Fainting at Fréjus

> *How do you save two people? I was so torn, I froze!*
> *I was so geared into listening for the numbers so I could save whoever was called,*
> *I forgot for a moment; it was my number. I needed saved!*
>
> —*Giving Voice* troupe members

Objective: Trust other members to catch you and keep others from falling.
When to use: After trust has been established and members are comfortable around each other.
Procedure:

- Have the troupe members number off.
- Ask them to just move around in the space close together, never moving too far from one another.
- Explain you are going to call out a number. The actor with the number called must "faint" and start falling. It is up to all the others to catch them before they fall to the floor. Encourage dramatic or slow faints, giving the members time to get to them.
- Start by saying one number at a time and later try a sequence of two or three numbers together.

Debriefing Fainting at Fréjus Topics

- Initial thoughts about what they just experienced
- Feeling responsible for keeping others safe
- Worrying that they might not be caught
- Relation to the troupe's work

Groups

> *Wow! Even we don't talk about some of this stuff. Talk about assumptions, even with movies. Of course, I guessed everyone was a poor college student.*
>
> —*Giving Voice* troupe member

Objective: Recognize assumptions and the effects
When to use: After the troupe is comfortable with each other and has developed an ensemble
Procedure:

- Instruct everyone they are going to move around the space without talking, sign language, gesturing, etc. You will call out a group, and everyone is to join that group. They must make the decision quickly and remember not to talk, gesture, or communicate in any way. They cannot ask you to clarify the group you call out. Explain you will count down from five to one. They must be in a group, even if alone, by the time you reach one.

- The following groups to call out will get you started. You can add or adjust to suit your troupe. They are basically in a risk order from low to high. What to watch for in Debrief is included:

  - Shoes *(type, color, laces...)*
  - Hair *(color, length, texture…)*
  - Tops *(blouse/shirt/t-shirt, color, design...)*
  - Movie preference *(many will have to make assumptions about the movies others like)*
  - Skin color *(actual color, racial based, bi-racial...)*
  - GPA *(many will make assumptions since most do not talk about GPA)*
  - Wealth *(assumptions again since most do not talk about socio-economic status)*
  - Politics *(assumptions again since most do not talk about politics)*
  - Religion *(many will make assumptions since most do not talk about religion)*

Debriefing Groups Topics

- Initial thoughts about what they just experienced
- What assumptions were made
- Someone being left out of a group
- How did that feel?
- Did they change to go along with a group rather than stand alone?
- How did it feel to stand alone?
- How did it feel to see someone standing alone?
- Why were there several groups possibly for religion and politics? (most did not know or want to assume, especially religion)
- What do we share or talk about? This may not be as unspoken with the troupe depending on how long they have had to get to know each other.
- Relation to the troupe's work

Privilege Walk

(edited from the Edward Ginsberg Center for Community Service and Learning)

> *I turned and saw how far back some of my friends were, especially compared to where I was.*
>
> *I just wanted to cry.*
>
> —cisgender white male *Giving Voice* troupe member

IMPORTANT: This exercise can be very triggering, so do not do this activity unless you are sure you have plenty of time to debrief and reflect on what individuals experienced during the privilege walk. There are many versions of this exercise, and you can adapt the version that works best for your situation. The following is one of the shorter versions.

Objective: Recognize the inequity of privilege
When to use: Later in the training, after there is solid trust among the troupe members
Procedure:

- Participants should be assured they may step out at any point, if needed. Participants stand in a straight line in the middle of an empty room. Tell them that some statements might be of a sensitive nature for some individuals, and that they do not have to respond to any statement that is uncomfortable. Read the statements below.

  If your ancestors came to the United States by force, take one step back.
  If you ever felt unsafe because of your sexual orientation, take one step back.
  If you believe that you were *denied employment* because of your race, gender, or ethnicity, take 1 step back.
  If you believe that you were *paid less* because of your race, gender, or ethnicity, take one step back.
  If you were ever stopped or questioned by the police because of your race, take one step back.
  If you ever felt uncomfortable about a joke directed at your gender or race, take one step back.
  If you can show affection for your romantic partner in public without fear of ridicule or violence, please take one step forward.
  If you were embarrassed about your clothes or house growing up, take one step back.
  If your parents or guardians attended college, take one step forward.
  If you were raised in an area with crime and drug activity, take one step back.
  If you have tried to change your speech or mannerisms to gain credibility, take one step back.
  If you are able to move through the world without fear of sexual assault, take one step forward.
  If you are reasonably sure that you will not be denied access to jobs or political resources because of your gender, take one step forward.
  If you are relatively sure you can enter a store without being followed, take one step forward.
  If you are reasonably sure you would be hired based on your ability and qualifications, take one step forward.

If your family automatically expected you to attend college, take one step forward.
If you have ever traveled outside the United States, take one step forward.
If your parents worked nights and weekends to support your family, take one step backward.
If you can buy new clothes or go out to dinner when you want to, take one step forward.
If you get time off for your religious holidays, take one step forward.
If you have a foreign accent, take one step backward.
If you can walk alone at any time of day or night without thinking about safety, take one step forward.
If you went to galleries, museums, and plays with your family, take one step forward.
If you attended private school or summer camp, take one step forward.
If you were raised in a single-parent household, take one step backward.
If you studied the culture of your ancestors in school, take one step forward.
If members of your gender are portrayed on TV in degrading roles, take one step backward.
If you have been a victim of sexual harassment, take one step backward.
If you have been a victim of violence because of your race, gender, class, or sexual orientation, take one step back.
If you ever went on a family vacation, take one step forward.
If you can walk on a sidewalk without being looked up and down or cat-called at, take one step forward.

Debriefing Privilege Walk Topics

Start by having everyone look at where everyone ended, including themselves. Circle up. You can start the debrief by asking the following questions:

- What is your "gut reaction" to where you found yourself at the end of this list?
- Are you surprised at where you are?
- How does it feel to be in front? Middle? Back?
- Did you come to any new realizations? If so, which one had the most impact?
- Encourage participants to share their experiences and feelings.
- Relation to the troupe's work

Other points to keep in mind:

This exercise is about privilege. Every statement addresses some small privilege that is based on gender, race, ethnicity, class, or sexual orientation. The small statements in this exercise have added up to divide people into different locations in this room. Similarly, small privileges in society place individuals in different places in society. This is systemic oppression.

Interestingly, privilege tends to be invisible to those who are privileged. That is, when we receive privilege based on race, gender, ethnicity, sexual orientation, or any other factor, we tend not to recognize the boosts in position that accumulate over time from those privileges.

The point of this exercise is not to make any of us embarrassed about the privileges we have received or do not have, but to make all of us aware of how privilege based on gender, race, etc., functions. Whether we are highly privileged, moderately privileged or lack privilege, it is possible to behave in ways that level the playing field for everyone.

IMAGES

> *I can't believe some of the things that popped into my head. I thought I was past that.*
>
> —*Giving Voice* troupe member

IMPORTANT: This exercise can be very triggering, so do not do this activity unless you are sure you have plenty of time to debrief and reflect on what individuals experienced during IMAGES.

Objective: Allow themselves to acknowledge what first comes to mind for the given image word, usually a stereotype, in order to better understand themselves and is needed for workshopping scripts.

When to use: After your troupe has established a significantly safe environment based on trust for each other.

Procedure:

Remind them of the rules they have adopted, especially to think the best of each other. This is very important as scripts are being improvised, including the oppressions that will come up in the moment. This exercise should help them to not overthink about what will look or sound bad to others and themselves. Instead, they are to go with what first comes to mind. Unfortunately, these will often be stereotypes and, in many cases, very offensive stereotypes, but that will become part of the *Debrief.*

- Remind troupe members they may step out at any time, if needed.
- Instruct them to stand in a circle with room to move with arms out.
- During the exercise they can move but are to stay in place.
- You will be saying an image to become.
- Then you will ask them to *dynamize* (movement and sound) their image or bring it to life.

- They will then add one movement and one sound to go with their image.
- They are to repeat the movement and sound until you say "freeze."
- You may ask them to stay in their frozen position, while also opening their eyes and looking at the other images.
- Then relax and go back to neutral to start the next image you say.
- Remind everyone to think the best of each other.
- Do not censor yourselves but go with first impulse.
- Protect yourself emotionally and mentally.

The following list starts with low risk and ends with higher-risk images. You can use all or some or add your own that are appropriate for your troupe.

Remind them to close their eyes.

- **BABY**

  Become a baby, without opening eyes and without movement

  1 Find the frozen image.
  2 DYNAMIZE it (repetitive sound and motion).
  3 FREEZE.
  4 Open eyes and look around at the other images.
  5 Close eyes and return to neutral.

  Remind them to remember rules, especially THINK THE BEST OF EACH OTHER, as you repeat this process with the words given. This can get intense, so be ready to give permission, if needed, to step out. I do not offer this until I detect it may be needed. Otherwise, some will opt out to avoid the hard work of this exercise. It could also be intimidating to be watched by non-participants.

  1 Find the frozen image.
  2 DYNAMIZE it (repetitive sound and motion).
  3 FREEZE.
  4 Open eyes and look around at the other images.
  5 Close eyes and return to neutral.

REPEAT the above five-step sequence with each of the following:

- **OPPRESSOR**
- **OPPRESSED**

If needed, remind "no talking" except during *dynamizing*.

- **WOMAN**
- **MAN**

Ask if everyone is okay with others seeing *dynamization.*

If all agree, have them open their eyes and look around at others during *dynamization.*

- **Gay**
- **Straight**
- **Muslim**
- **Native American**
- **Asian**
- **Black**
- **Latinx**
- **Native American**
- **White/Caucasian**
- **Sexism**
- **Homophobia**
- **Racism**

Debriefing Images Topics

- Start by checking in to make sure everyone is okay and ready to discuss
- Initial thoughts about what they just experienced and willing to share
- What first came to mind?
- Were you surprised? Did you change?
- Relation to the troupe's work

There will be a wide variety of reactions to this exercise. This will run from hurt seeing how their community is depicted to hurt from the realization of privilege. Discussion should include the shame some may have felt because of what came to mind first. Some even allowed their impulse to change their first reaction to something less hurtful. Remind them that no one is perfect. We are the sum of our experiences, influences, and lack thereof. We cannot control our initial thoughts, but we can control our next actions or words.

Continue Building

> *I am so grateful to have Giving Voice to discuss issues.*
> *Most teachers avoid these types of discussions.*
>
> —*Giving Voice* troupe member

By this point, the troupe will have made great progress in becoming an ensemble. The space is safe to share and discuss a variety of topics and improv scenarios. At this point, you can continue to use Boal games or other exercises. This will depend on how much time you have since you are also developing scripts and preparing for forums. At this point, it is encouraged to use simple fun games, even childhood games to counter the seriousness of most of the work. Troupe members can also contribute by leading their favorite game.

References

Boal, A. (1992). *Games for actors and non-actors* (A. Jackson, Trans.). Routledge.

Privilege Walk. (2023, June 21). Csmedia1.com. https://www.csmedia1.com/mxchurch.org/privilege-walk-activity.pdf

4 Script Development

Troupe Members as Researchers

"Asking people to share their stories of oppression was intimidating at first. Then I realized many wanted to talk about it and let others know what is going on" (*Giving Voice* troupe member). While engaged in the various ensemble-building endeavors and *Theatre of the Oppressed* exercises to prepare them for this type of work, the troupe members must also become researchers. Their ongoing assignment is to gather true stories of oppression from their campus and share those stories in rehearsals. They will have no trouble finding stories.

Gathering Stories

The overarching question the troupe members are asking is for someone to share their story of how they have been oppressed in class, the hall, walking across campus, etc. For most, the initial answer is to say they have not been oppressed. The word "oppressed" conjures the most egregious acts or words. Troupe members have found it more useful to start the conversation by asking someone if they have ever felt uncomfortable because of something someone said or did. This goes back to microaggressions seeming small and therefore not shared, even though they can be very harmful. Once someone recognizes that these are microaggressions that have hurt them mentally and emotionally, they open up to the interviewer. If the troupe is developing a script for their own environment, they often already know the people they interview. Already having that bond will make it easier. Ask for permission to record the interview, so nothing is missed, and it can be transcribed later. Even though the easiest way to keep track is by recording, the identity of all persons interviewed is to be protected.

The following are good questions to choose from for an interview. Be sure to just listen for the majority of the interview. You can start with the basics: Who, What, When, Where, and Why.

Who said or did something offensive? (This in reference to position such as teacher, classmate, friend, not the name of the person)

What happened?

DOI: 10.4324/9781032676883-4

When did it happen?
Where did it happen?
Why do you think it happened?

Other possible questions or prompts:

Tell me a little about yourself.
Describe a situation where you felt uncomfortable.
When that happened, how did it make you feel?
What did you do or say?
How was what you said received?
Why did you not say anything?
Do you want someone to stand up for you?
Has there been a time someone stood up for you?
How did it feel to have someone else say something for you?
What would you like others to do to help?
Have there been other incidents?
How do these incidents affect you past the incident?

Scenario

I am not light enough for the whites and not dark enough for the Blacks.
— *Giving Voice* Troupe member

The stories that are gathered can often serve a dual purpose, depending on your audience. For example, in a school or college setting, the script can be used for both student forums and faculty development forums with minor adjustments. The charge for the original *Giving Voice* Project was professional development for faculty and administration, emphasizing racial diversity challenges. Again, this was in response to the *Voices of Diversity* (2009) report. Therefore, the majority of the stories came from classrooms and campuses. It also became clear we needed one more member in the troupe to play the teacher in what was developing as a classroom scenario. A graduate assistant joined the troupe to help with the improv and play the role of teacher. Since then, forums have been very successful with undergraduate students in more mature roles, such as teachers or business managers.

Script Development from True Personal Narratives

Developing the actual scripts to use in forums is a series of improvisations based on the interviews and your troupe's personal experiences. After a brief warmup and possibly one or two Boal games, circle up the troupe for script discussions.

Interviews

Start by troupe members sharing what they have found out in their interviews.

Quotes

Especially look for quotes that can be used by the characters in the scenario. It may be helpful to display some of those quotes and make it a goal to work those into the improv for the script. It is also good to let audiences know that the most egregious comments they are about to hear were not made up for the effect but are verbatim, what has been said to someone.

Script Improvisation

It might be helpful to establish a setting, such as a classroom, a study group, or the cafeteria, but it is also okay to decide on the setting once the script starts taking form. If you have several members in the troupe, it might be good to split them up and have each group work on improvising a script.

Improv Groups

Diverse troupe members will most likely make up the final cast for the script, and it is a good way to divide the troupe for improv. However, allowing troupe members who might have similar experiences can reveal topics that might be overlooked otherwise. Not everyone has experienced the same microaggressions. Also, there are struggles within communities, such as a biracial person not feeling they are accepted by either race.

Improvisation

Give groups about 20–30 minutes to use highlights from their interviews to start developing a scenario with dialogue. Watch for groups that may tend to sit and discuss the interviews and possible options, rather than improvising the scenario's possibilities. While a short discussion is helpful, encourage them to get up and act out their discussion and thoughts. Many, including trained actors, are hesitant to do actual improvisation, but once they are up and moving, the ideas come much faster and are more relevant. They can use their phones to record and transcribe later.

Build from Improv: After time to improv in groups, bring everyone back together to present what they have developed. After each group has presented, it is time to build. Select one group to go again, only this time others can enter as another character when they have an idea that is sparked by something in the presentation. Another option is to have two groups try to combine the basics from each one. Be sure to record the improvs to develop an outline for the next rehearsal.

Outline: Building off the improv from the last rehearsal, start to put together an outline of a script (see Appendix D). This can include dialogue developed that already seems to work. In addition, add directions for the next improv. These can be a general directive such as "talk about the assignment and include an inappropriate question about someone's background." Since part of the script is already structured, it can guide the next phase of improv. Soon you want to decide character names and include the names in the script. This will help troupe members take on the characters and help the audience learn names.

Repeat: Continue to workshop the true stories, using improvisation and exercises, and each newly evolved outline (see Appendix E) until a short scenario is developed. Record and transcribe from the last improv at each rehearsal in order to tighten the outline until it becomes a script. This is done several times with continuous editing and refining of the transcriptions until there is a scenario for a forum. Although this could take several attempts, find a stopping place for a good script, knowing you can still edit. Scenarios should run about six to seven minutes and not exceed 10 minutes. Although tempting, do not try to fit everything into the script. There will be other ways to bring up issues not in the script, namely with *Talking Points* during the *Talkbacks*. The script is like a painting, which according to Paul Gardner, "… is never finished – it simply stops in interesting places" (Bohn, 2023). You need to find that interesting stopping place when you have covered issues and have developed characters. There is not always a definitive brush stroke, especially with new examples constantly happening in the world. Basically, when you have covered the most important issues at the time, then you are ready to further develop the characters. Character development can cause small changes in the script, so be open to adjustments.

***Address the Issues*:** Remember the scenario is designed to address the topics of microaggressions including stereotyping and other forms of oppression. Microaggressions are part of casual conversations, a little joke or comment, or sometimes a single word that has made it into our vernacular. People who experience themselves as good, moral, and decent human beings who would never intentionally discriminate against others often perpetrate these small oppressions. Microaggressions cut across all social identities including race, ethnicity, religion, nationality, sexual orientation, gender identity, gender expression, age, disability status, socio-economic class, and other important social dimensions. These insults and invalidations occur throughout organizations, including all majors, departments, and colleges in a university.

***Tips*:** Do not avoid subtext. Part of becoming aware of oppression is to watch actions, as well as words. Watch out for being too overt. An assumption is better than an explicit statement. An example might be when a character says, “And I’m Puerto Rican and black, not white and black.” She might say instead, “What makes you think I’m Black and white?” Not everything should be vague but enough should be omitted to force audience members into making assumptions about the characters. As in actual situations, this will have the audience question themselves rather than spelling everything out (i.e., Is he gay or not? What race is she? Is he sexist or not? Does he have a problem with gay people or is he just joking around?). Keep the setting vague. Not everyone can transfer bigotry from one setting to another. Also, audience members may try to avoid engagement by asking about the class assignment, curriculum, classroom management techniques, or business products. This helps avoid fact that these oppressions happen in any setting, and the purpose of the forum is to recognize and then address these oppressions.

Bigotry is seldom overt in most settings you will be addressing. If too overt, the audience might find the scenario a bit unrealistic, and the perceived realism of the scenario can affect what audience members get out of the experience. Some of that overtness can be solved by having the characters make statements as asides, where a character might make a racist or other overt or derogatory comment to another character, not meaning to be overheard, even if he is.

A final tip would be to keep the scenario under ten minutes and that can be long. Shorter scenes work better for audience attention spans, especially if they do not really want to be there in the first place.

Final Script

The result of the *Giving Voice* Project’s first script was a scenario titled *American History* (see Appendix F). Set in a college history class, a new instructor struggles with the challenges of diverse students. After being given a group assignment to look at a current event from a historical perspective, the students in the scenario begin to brainstorm ideas. This free exchange of ideas becomes a problem for some students and uncomfortable for most, due to comments made during the discussion. For instance, one student suggests using President Obama’s election as the topic. Based on what had been said about 2008 candidate Obama, a troupe member added during an improv, “You know, how he got the black vote because he’s black, but he also got the white vote because he’s light-skinned and doesn’t sound like a black person.”

This statement instigates a series of reactions and comments. The instructor tries to intervene saying they can relate and tells a story about being invited to a step competition. However, the teacher’s focus is on the students of color. The story concludes with, “I looked around. I found I was the only white person there and I thought, Oh, I’m the minority. This is what it feels like to be a minority. And you know I learned from it. I have grown as a person, and now I have Black friends. I even invite some of them over for dinner.” Needless to say, this simplification of racism (which actually occurred) in a college classroom, does not help the situation.

The script should shine a light on the issues without resolving them. If you address them in the script with strong characters that are not afraid to speak up for themselves, then there is nothing for the audience to learn to recognize and how to intervene. The rest of the forum is for addressing these issues. While creating the scenario to be used in a forum workshop, the troupe members also develop characters to bring different perspectives or voices to the forum. These characters are then fully developed with complete backstories and their own voices that influence them.

References

Bohn. (2023, March 28). *Paul Gardner — 'A painting is never finished* [Video]. YouTube. https://www.youtube.com/watch?v=3oAjZ1L1yWo

Caplan, P., Nettles, M., Millett, C., Miller, S., DiCrecchio, N., & Chu, T. (2009). The voices of diversity: What racial/ethnic minority students can tell us about advantages and disadvantages of attending predominantly white colleges. *Preliminary Report for Missouri State University*. 1–74

Appendix D

Scenario #1 (American History)

SAM enters and sits in seat #1. She takes out homework from another class and starts working on it.

DREW enters and puts books in seat #6 (where he usually sits). Rather than sitting down, however, he goes up to Sam and sits in seat #2 to talk to her. He asks is she's in his other class. He asks if she understood a word of the lecture (the instructor is from another country and speaks with an accent).

SAM tells him she is in the class and that all the information from the lecture is in the book.

DREW thanks her and stands to move back to his seat, but stops when DANNIE, KANOME, and ROLO enter.

DANNIE, KANOME, and ROLO enter before DREW has a chance to move back to his seat. They are talking about the new *TWILIGHT* movie. DANNIE has seen it, but the other two have not. DANNIE sits backward in seat #3.

KANOME sits in seat #5.

ROLO stands while leaning on seat #4.

DREW asks what movie they are talking about (if it isn't clear from the conversation). He makes a comment to the effect of "Yeah … you only want to see it because of the hot half-naked 'Indian boys'" on his way back to his seat (#6). He includes ROLO in this comment … making a thinly veiled reference to his sexuality.

ARIEL enters on this comment and sits in seat #7.

KANOME corrects him to the effect of, "First, they aren't 'Indian boys' … they are 'native american men.' Second, yes they are very attractive." KANOME and DANNIE give each other a high five or some other sign of solidarity.

DREW calls her a "pig" with feigned indignation and sits in seat #6.

ARIEL says something to the effect of, "No, they want to see it because it represents every girl's 'fairy tale' dream."

DANNIE blows him off and calls him a "retard" before turning around to sit in her seat.

ROLO notices that seat #2 is empty and asks something to the effect of, "Where's the Asian girl … What's her name?"

Knowing that this isn't her name, DREW tells him something to the effect of "I think it's Ling Ling, isn't it?" (asking ARIEL to play along with the joke).

ARIEL says something to the effect of "Yeah, I think that's right."

The TEACHER enters and moves to her desk to put down her books, etc.

ROLO sees the TEACHER and sits in his chair saying something to the effect of "Well, she better show up today. She gave me her notes yesterday, and I can't make heads or tails out of them … they just look like a bunch of 'wing dings'."

The TEACHER greets the class, calling them 'boys and girls.' She makes a bit of small talk ("How is everyone?" etc.) before moving on to the day's work.

The TEACHER gives them the following information: The other groups have already chosen their topics for the group presentation so they have the day to go to the library to research (The assignment is to look at a current event from a historical perspective). As soon as this group chooses a topic and gets it okayed by her they may do the same. Before they get started, though she makes a list of who is in the group. She doesn't know their names yet … so she asks them to call them out to her. She asks if anyone is missing.

KANOME tells her that "Ling Ling," the "oriental" girl, isn't there.

The TEACHER, thinking she is making a racist comment, corrects her. She says something to the effect of "She isn't 'oriental' … I think she's actually Chinese. And while 'Ling Ling' is a Chinese name … It's the name of a panda. Her name happens to be 'Li Ming'."

KANOME tries to clear things up, but the TEACHER (clearly irritated) blows her off and tells the group to get to work. She then takes out a stack of papers and starts grading them. The students move their chairs into a pseudo semi-circle.

SAM asks the TEACHER if they can choose a topic without LI MING's presence.

The TEACHER tells them to go ahead, saying something to the effect of "She'll catch up … I've yet to have an 'asian' who wasn't at the top of the class.

ARIEL makes a smart-aleck remark about what the TEACHER just said.

DANNIE (playing a trick on DREW and ARIEL) says something to the effect of "You guys are really rude. You know my grandmother happens to be Chinese."

ARIEL and DREW are taken aback. ARIEL says something to the effect of "Really?"

DANNIE says something to the effect of "No, idiot, do I look Chinese" and points to her eyes.

SAM, not realizing that she's being rude asks something to the effect of "What are you?"

DANNIE tells her that she's half African-American and half Puerto Rican.

DREW tells her something to the effect of "Then you're black."

DANNIE says something to the effect of "No, I'm bi-racial."

DREW tells her that society sees her as black just like Obama … that's how he got elected. He got the black vote because society sees him as black, but he got the white vote because he's light skinned and doesn't sound like a black person.

KANOME responds in outrage.

The TEACHER looks up. The argument continues briefly until the TEACHER interrupts, telling KANOME to hold it down and get back to work (thinking that she's the one who started it).

ROLO tries to make peace within the group.

SAM agrees saying that they should really get to work and that this conversation has nothing to do with the assignment.

ARIEL asks why not? Why can't they talk about the election?

ROLO says something to the effect of "I guess we could. We could talk about how he hasn't made good on any of his promises to any 'minority' in America … he's done nothing about 'Don't Ask Don't Tell' or the 'Defense of Marriage Act' (This comment is based on the gay community's dissatisfaction with Obama's treatment of gay rights).

KANOME tells him that the term 'minority' isn't politically correct because it denotes that various groups are "less than …" She says that the preferred term is 'people of color'.

ROLO tells her that that's ridiculous because it totally leaves out other groups based on religion or sexual orientation.

The TEACHER who has been keeping one eye on the group since her interruption comes over to stand behind seat #2 and asks if they are getting close to choosing a topic yet.

SAM tells her that they are thinking about discussing how the fact that Obama is bi-racial helped him get elected.

The TEACHER says something to the effect of "That's right, isn't it? His father was black and his mother was white, weren't they? (Speaking to DANNIE) What is it with black men and white women?"

DANNIE shrugs.

ARIEL, having a sudden idea, says something to the effect of "We could also talk about how the fact that he's Muslim played a role."

DREW (to ARIEL) says something to the effect of "He wasn't Muslim … He was Baptist. (He turns to Kanome) Right?

KANOME, who is thoroughly disgusted with this class by now, explodes to the effect of "Why are you asking me? Do you think that just because I'm black I automatically know the religion of every other black person in America?" The class erupts in chaos.

ROLO tries to smooth things over.

DANNIE takes KANOME's side.

ARIEL takes DREW's side.

SAM tries to get them focused back on the presentation.

The TEACHER interrupts by shouting KANOME's name until she gets everyone's attention. She then very harshly says something to KANOME to the effect of "Zip it!" She then tells the group to get back to work and goes back to her desk shaking her head. The group sits in silence for a moment.

SAM tentatively asks, "So, are we going to talk about Obama or not?"

THE END

Appendix E

Scenario #3 (American History)

SAM enters and sits in seat #1. She takes out homework from another class and starts working on it.

DREW enters and puts books in seat #6 (where he usually sits). Rather than sitting down, however, he goes up to Sam and sits in seat #2 to talk to her. He asks is she's in his other class. He asks if she understood a word of the lecture (then indicates the problem is instructor is from another country and speaks with an accent ~ "learn plain English"/needs an American teacher).

SAM tells him she is in the class and that all the information from the lecture is in the book.

DREW thanks her and stands to move back to his seat, but stops when DANNIE and ROLO enter.

DANNIE and ROLO enter before DREW has a chance to move back to his seat. They are talking about the new *TWILIGHT* movie. DANNIE has seen it, but Rolo has not. DANNIE sits backward in seat #4.

ROLO stands while leaning on seat #5.

DREW asks what movie they are talking about (if it isn't clear from the conversation). He makes a comment to the effect of "Yeah … you only want to see it because of the hot half-naked 'Indian boys'" on his way back to his seat (#6). He includes ROLO in this comment … making a thinly veiled reference to his sexuality.

KANOME enters. She starts talking before they get to their seats (She sits in seat #3). She says something to the effect of "What's up with all those Muslim guys by the front door?"

DANNIE says something to the effect of "Who?"

ROLO says something to the effect of "We didn't come in that way."

SAM says something to the effect of "Yeah, I saw them. They kind of freaked me out a little bit."

KANOME says something to the effect of "That's not what I meant. I wasn't afraid they were wearing an underwear bomb or anything." KANOME sits in seat #4.

DREW says something to the effect of "What did you mean? And what makes you think they were Muslim anyway?"

KANOME says something to the effect of "Well, they were Middle-Eastern."

DREW says something to the effect of "And all Middle-Easterners are automatically Muslim, I suppose."

SAM asks something to the effect of "Aren't they?"

DREW (playing a trick on SAM) says something to the effect of "Why don't you ask ARIEL when he gets here. He's Arabic."

SAM says something to the effect of "Is he really?"

****

ARIEL enters and in an exaggerated Middle-Eastern accent says something to the effect of "What are you talking about? I'm not Middle-Eastern." He drops the accent and adds, "I'm Puerto Rican." ARIEL sits in seat #7.

DREW laughs at the joke played on Sam et al.

DANNIE tells KANOME something like "this guy (DREW) thinks we like *TWILIGHT* because of the hot half-naked Indian boys."

KANOME corrects him to the effect of, "First, they aren't 'Indian boys' … they are 'native American men.' Second, yes they are very attractive." KANOME and DANNIE give each other a high five or some other sign of solidarity.

ARIEL says something to the effect of, "No, they want to see it because it represents every girl's 'fairy tale' dream.

DANNIE blows him off and calls him a 'retard' before turning around to sit in her seat.

ROLO notices that seat #2 is empty and asks something to the effect of, "Where's the Asian girl … What's her name?"

Knowing that this isn't her name, DREW tells him something to the effect of "I think it's Ling Ling, isn't it?" (asking ARIEL to play along with the joke).

ARIEL says something to the effect of "Yeah, I think that's right."

ROLO says something to the effect of "Well, I hope she shows up today. She gave me her notes yesterday, and I can't make heads or tails out of them … they just look like a bunch of 'wing dings'.

****

The TEACHER enters and moves to her desk to put down her books, etc. She greets the class, calling them 'boys and girls.' She makes a bit of small talk ("How is everyone?" etc.) as she takes out the class roster. She asks who is missing.

KANOME tells her that 'Ling Ling', the 'oriental' girl, isn't there.

The TEACHER, thinking she is making a racist comment, corrects her. She says something to the effect of "She isn't 'oriental' … I think she's actually Chinese. And while 'Ling Ling' is a Chinese name … it's the name of a panda. Her name happens to be 'Li Ming'.

KANOME tries to clear things up, but the TEACHER (clearly irritated) blows her off and (using "guys" to get the students attention) gives them the following information: The other groups have already chosen their topics for the group presentation so they have the day to go to the library to research (The assignment is to look at a current event from an historical perspective). As soon as this group chooses a topic and gets it okayed by her they may do the same. Before they get started, though she makes a list of who is in the group. She doesn't know their names yet … so she asks them to call them out to her. She then takes out a stack of papers and starts grading them. The students move their chairs into a pseudo semi-circle.

****

SAM asks the TEACHER if they can choose a topic without LI MING's presence.

The TEACHER tells them to go ahead, saying something to the effect of "She'll catch up … I've yet to have an 'asian' who wasn't at the top of the class.

ARIEL makes a smart-aleck remark about what the TEACHER just said.

DANNIE (playing a trick on DREW and ARIEL) says something to the effect of "You guys are really rude. You know my grandmother happens to be Chinese."

ARIEL and DREW are taken aback. ARIEL says something to the effect of "Really?"

DANNIE says something to the effect of "No, idiot, do I look Chinese" and points to her eyes.

SAM, not realizing that she's being rude asks something to the effect of "What are you?"

DANNIE tells her that she's half African-American and half Puerto Rican.

DREW tells her something to the effect of "Then you're black."

DANNIE says something to the effect of "No, I'm bi-racial."

DREW tells her that society sees her as black just like Obama … that's how he got elected. He got the black vote because society sees him as black, but he got the white vote because he's light skinned and doesn't sound like a black person.

KANOME responds in outrage, including something to the effect of "That's so racist."

The TEACHER looks up. The argument continues briefly until the TEACHER interrupts, telling KANOME to hold it down and get back to work (thinking that she's the one who started it).

****

ROLO tries to make peace within the group.

SAM agrees saying that they should really get to work and that this conversation has nothing to do with the assignment.

ARIEL asks "Why not? Why can't we talk about the election? It's a current event.

DREW says something to the effect of "Because that's racist. I guess I am in good company since President Obama has been called racist, too."

KANOME says something to the effect of "Obama can't be racist because he's an African American."

DREW asks KANOME something to the effect of "So … only whites can be racist?"

KANOME asks DREW something to the effect of "How have 'your people' been victimized?"

DREW says something to the effect of "'Your people?'" He then adds in a stereotypical African-American dialect, "I know you gotta be tight wit da family tree, but … what?"

KANOME asks DREW if he has any idea how racist what he just said is.

ARIEL says something to the effect of "Okay, Double-standard Debbie … You talk like a stereotypical white person. Does that make you a racist?

DREW tells KANOME something to the effect of "And yes … I have been victimized … by every liberal leftist instructor who seems to think that white men are the cause of all the world's problems." He goes on to emphasize this fact by saying that he has never owned slaves or denied women the right to vote.

SAM says something to the effect of "Yeah. I get made fun of all the time because I'm from a small town." She then encourages them to get to work and something to the effect of "how about we just stick to Obama's policies?"

ROLO says something to the effect of "I guess we could. We could talk about how he hasn't made good on any of his promises to any 'minority' in America … he's done nothing about 'Don't Ask Don't Tell' or the 'Defense of Marriage Act'

KANOME tells him that the term 'minority' isn't politically correct because it denotes that various groups are "less than …" She says that the preferred term is 'people of color'.

ROLO tells her that that's ridiculous because that it totally leaves out other groups based on religion or sexual orientation.

****

TEACHER who has been keeping one eye on the group since her interruption comes over to stand behind seat #3 and "relates with something to the effect of "I was just like you (meaning DREW and SAM) when I was an undergrad, until this African-American girl invited me to a student step competition. Everyone was very nice and friendly, but I felt out of place. When I looked around, I realized I was the only white person there and I thought, 'Oh my god … I'm the minority here. This is what it feels like to be a minority.' Now, some of my best friends are black … I even invited her to my wedding."

ROLO says "It's just like the song from that musical: (*singing)* Everyone's a little bit racist."

ARIEL says "Dude, could you be any gayer?"

TEACHER asks if they are getting close to choosing a topic yet.

SAM tells her that they are thinking about discussing how the fact that Obama is bi-racial helped him get elected.

TEACHER says something to the effect of "That's right, isn't it? His father was black and his mother was white, weren't they? (Speaking to DANNIE) What is it with black men and white women?"

DANNIE shrugs.

ARIEL, having a sudden idea, says something to the effect of "We could also talk about how the fact that he's Muslim played a role."

DREW (to ARIEL) says something to the effect of "He wasn't Muslim … He was Baptist. (He turns to Kanome) Right?

KANOME, who is thoroughly disgusted with this class by now, explodes to the effect of "Why are you asking me? Do you think that just because I'm black I automatically know the religion of every other black person in America?" The class erupts in chaos.

ROLO tries to smooth things over.

DANNIE takes KANOME's side.

ARIEL takes DREW's side.

SAM tries to get them focused back on the presentation.

The TEACHER interrupts by shouting KANOME's name until she gets everyone's attention. She then very harshly says something to KANOME to the effect of "Zip it!" She then tells the group to get back to work and goes back to her desk shaking her head. The group sits in silence for a moment.

SAM tentatively asks "So, are we going to talk about Obama or not?"

THE END

Appendix F

Giving Voice (American History)

(*ANGIE enters and sits in seat #1. She takes out homework from another class and starts working on it.*)

(*BRANDON enters and puts books in seat #6. He does not sit.)*

BRANDON: Hey! Are you in that computer class with me? … Right before this?

ANGIE: Dr. Cho?

BRANDON: Yeah. (H*e goes up to ANGIE and sits in seat #2 to talk to her.*)

ANGIE, right?

ANGIE: Yeah

BRANDON: Brandon. Could you follow that lecture? I can't understand a word he says.

ANGIE: (*Chuckle*) No…and when he writes it just looks like a bunch of wing dings to me.

BRANDON: (*Laughing*) I know, right?

ANGIE: But seriously, everything he does is straight out of the book…I have a friend who had him last semester. If you just read along with the syllabus you'll be fine.

BRANDON: Cool. Good to know. Thanks.

ANGIE: Sure.

(*REBECCA and ALEJANDRO enter. REBECCA will sit in seat #5. ALEJANDRO will lean on seat #3.)*

REBECCA: (*In the middle of a conversation*) No. The special effects were horrible. But we also rented the latest "Twilight" movie. You have to see it.

ALEJANDRO: Was it good?

REBECCA: It *definitely* had its moments.

BRANDON: (*Standing*) Yeah…you guys just want to see it because of the half-naked Indian boys. (*He crosses US of them to seat #6*)

REBECCA: Okay…first of all they aren't "Indians, "they are "Native Americans." And that was only *one* of the reasons that I liked it.

BRANDON: Why *else* could you possibly have liked it? The books were *crap.*

ALEJANDRO: They were not!

BRANDON: The only reason why any girl likes that is the fantasy. You all just want some guy to come in and sweep you off your feet. (*ALEJANDRO sits*)

REBECCA: Whatever. You're an idiot. (*She turns around to face away from BRANDON*)

(*LENNON enters. She crosses to SL of seat #7)*

ALEJANDRO: Hey, Lennon.

LENNON: Hey, Alejandro…Do you guys know what's up with all the Muslim guys by the front door?

ALEJANDRO: (*Shakes his head*) We didn't come in that way. Why?

LENNON: Oh…I just thought it was really strange.

ANGIE: Yeah, I did too. It kind of freaked me out a little bit.

LENNON: (*Crosses US of desks to seat #4 and puts down her stuff, but remains standing*) No, I didn't mean that. I just thought it was odd they were congregating around the door. I wasn't afraid they were going to bomb us or anything. (*Turning to BRANDON*) Did you see them?

BRANDON: No. What makes you think they were Muslim anyway?

LENNON: They had those *things* on their heads. (*pantomimes a turban*)

BRANDON: A turban? They were Muslim because they were wearing turbans?

LENNON: Well, they were Middle Eastern.

BRANDON: So all Middle Easterners are Muslim?

LENNON: (*Looking around for support*) Aren't they?

BRANDON: I don't know. (*Indicating MALIK's empty chair*) Why don't you ask Malik when he gets here? I think he's Arabic.

ANGIE: Is he really?

ALEJANDRO: No he's not. Is he? (*BRANDON nods*)

(*The TEACHER enters and crosses to her desk*)

TEACHER: Okay. Sorry. I'm a little late, so we don't really have time for chit-chat today. (*Directed to LENNON*) Could everyone take a seat please? (*Looking around*) Who's missing?

ANGIE: I think just that Middle Eastern guy.

TEACHER: Who? (*Checking the roster*) Malik?

ANGIE: Yeah. I think so. He sits back…

(*MALIK enters on ANGIE's line and interrupts her*)

MALIK: (*In an exaggerated Middle Eastern accent*) What are you talking about? I'm not Middle Eastern. (*He drops the accent*) I'm Puerto Rican.

ALEJANDRO: Oh my god! That has to be the *worst* accent I've ever heard. You sound like you should be working in a convenience store.

TEACHER: Okay…settle down. Let's get back on topic. Thank you. Now, the other groups in the class have already chosen topics for their group presentations and are at the library doing research. What I need you guys to do today is get together and choose a topic. Remember…the assignment is to look at a current event from an historical perspective. In other words, think about how future history books will describe this event. Once you get your topic approved by me we'll all go over to the library and meet up with the other groups. Do you guys understand? Rebecca? (*Although the question is to the class, she is looking directly at REBECCA. The class nods, etc.*) Okay. You can move your chairs, but make sure you put them back before you leave. (*She goes to her desk, takes out a stack of papers and starts grading them. The students move their chairs into a pseudo semi-circle.*)

ANGIE: So…what do you guys want to do?

ALEJANDRO: I don't care.

BRANDON: We could talk about Obama being the first black president. You know, how he got elected…that he got the black vote because he's black, but he also got the white vote because he's light-skinned and doesn't sound like a black person.

REBECCA: Excuse me?!?!

LENNON: Okay. Obama is *not* black. He's bi-racial.

MALIK: It's the same thing. His skin tone is black.

LENNON: No. He's lighter skin-toned because he's bi-racial. When a person tells you they are more than one race, then they are bi-racial. You need to take into account that maybe it's not one of those, "Oh, yeah, she's black" or "Oh, no, she's not." Not all things are that simple.

REBECCA: (*Agreeing with LENNON*) Really!

BRANDON: I'm just saying his race/helped him get elected.

ALEJANDRO: (*Overlapping from* "race")/I just think Lennon's saying that you shouldn't ignore/the part of her that isn't black.

REBECCA: (*Overlapping from* "ignore")/I hate that argument anyway./That's not why he got elected. What? Do you think all the black people in America just stuck together to elect one of their own?

TEACHER: (*Overlapping from* "anyway." *The line* "REBECCA!!" *should roughly correspond with* "America")/Guys! ... Guys! ... Rebecca!!! (*After REBECCA is silent*) Keep it down. And get back to work.

(*Pause*)

LENNON: All I'm saying is that part of the time you don't think about what you're saying. You say, "Oh, you're black." No! I'm not *just* black, and neither is Obama.

ANGIE: What are you then?

LENNON: I'm Puerto Rican *and* black.

ANGIE: Oh. (*Pause*) Well, do we want to talk about *that* then?

MALIK: We could talk about how Obama has been called a racist. I think that's pretty interesting considering he's "bi-racial."

REBECCA: That's retarded. Obama's not a racist. He's a person of color.

BRANDON: So...only white people can be racist? Is that what you're saying?

KANOMOE: Oh?...you tell me how your people have been victimized through history.

BRANDON: Your people? (*In a stereotypical black dialect*) I know you gotta be tight wit da family tree and all, but...*your people*?!?!

REBECCA: Do you have any idea how racist what you just said was?

MALIK: Hold on, hold on! Just a minute! Just because he did the stereotypical ghetto slang he's racist?!?! Come on, you do it too. You talk like the stereotypical white person. Does that make you a racist?

BRANDON: For your information I have been victimized by every single, liberal, leftist professor who thinks that white men are the cause of all the world's problems. I've never owned slaves. I've never stopped women from voting.

ANGIE: Yeah. I'm always getting a hard time about being from a small town. That doesn't make me a racist...or ignorant...or anything like that.

REBECCA: (*to ANGIE*) Oh, you poor thing. You must have been so oppressed all your life.

ALEJANDRO: Okay. This isn't getting us anywhere. How about we just stick to his policies?

ANGIE: What do you mean?

ALEJANDRO: We could discuss all the promises he's made…how he took political stands on things…how the economy is horrible…gay marriage.

BRANDON: Knew that one would get brought up.

ALEJANDRO: Don't even start!

ANGIE: But we have to do it from a historical perspective.

ALEJANDRO: Well…he's historically not doing *anything* he promised… (*aimed at BRANDON*) for *any* minority.

REBECCA: You shouldn't use the word "minority."

MALIK: (*To BRANDON*) Here we go again.

REBECCA: Well, you shouldn't. It denotes that various groups are "less than. "You should use 'people of color.'

ALEJANDRO: What about the people who are gay? Buddhist? Muslim? What about them? Aren't they minorities?

REBECCA: I'm just telling you what the politically correct term is.

MALIK: Nobody talks in PC terms any more.

REBECCA: How did you even get into this institution?

(*The TEACHER who has been keeping one eye on the group since her interruption comes over to stand SL of ANGIE*)

TEACHER: I hear a lot of talking. Are we close to having some sort of topic chosen or what?

ANGIE: We were actually discussing, maybe, Obama. How being bi-racial helped him get elected.

BRANDON: Yeah. Pretty much.

TEACHER: Okay…because he is bi-racial, right? His father was black and his mother was white. You know, that was *very* unusual back then. Things have changed a *lot*. It's changed quite a bit even since I was an undergrad. I was from a small town like you (*Indicates ANGIE*), and when I was a junior I met an African-American student who invited me to one of those 'step competitions.' (*To LENNON and REBECCA*) Is that what it's called?

LENNON: I don't know. Do you mean…?

TEACHER: (*To REBECCA*) *You* know what I'm talking about, don't you?

REBECCA: Yeah. Go ahead.

TEACHER: Well, I went to this 'step competition,' and I was having a wonderful time. Everyone was very polite to me, but I felt a little out of place. I looked around. I found I was the only white person there. I thought, "Oh, I'm the minority. This is what it feels like to be a minority." And you know I learned from it. I have grown as a person, and now I have lots of black friends. I even invite some of them over. I truly believe that change is possible with tolerance. (*Pause*) And now just look…we even have a black president.

BRANDON: See? I told you he was black.

TEACHER: Okay…okay. Get back to work, (*almost an after-thought*) but I like where this is going.

(*Pause. LENNON, REBECCA, and ALEJANDRO look at each other.*)

LENNON: (*In disbelief*) Wow.

ALEJANDRO: (*talking about the TEACHER*) Well, you know…It's just like that song: (*singing*) "Everyone's a little bit racist."

ANGIE: *What* song?

ALEJANDRO: From the musical? … *Avenue Q*?

BRANDON: Dude, could you be any gayer?

(*ALEJANDRO is about to verbally attack BRANDON, but MALIK speaks first*)

MALIK: Hey! We could also talk about how the fact that he's Muslim played a role in the election.

BRANDON: (*to MALIK*) He wasn't even Muslim, was he?

ALEJANDRO: What are you talking about?

BRANDON: The media screwed it up or something. (*He turns to REBECCA*) He was Baptist, wasn't he?

REBECCA: Do I know? No! I don't know! Should I know telepathically the religion of every black person in America?!?!

(*Overlapping. REBECCA and BRANDON are arguing. LENNON and MALIK are arguing. ANGIE and ALEJANDRO interject over the two arguments. REBECCA should be the last person speaking.*)

ALEJANDRO: I don't think that's what he meant, Rebecca.

BRANDON: (*to REBECCA*) Why do you have to take everything so racial?

ANGIE: Can we please focus on the assignment?

LENNON: (*to BRANDON and MALIK*) You know, we only got into this argument because the first thing you two said was that Obama was racist.

REBECCA: (*to BRANDON*) Because you looked at me when you asked that question.

MALIK: (*to LENNON*) I didn't say that. You two think you have been through so much just because you are of a different color. You don't know what the rest of us have been through. You don't know what the rest of us have seen. Just because you have a different skin tone doesn't mean you're any better… any more a victim than the rest of us.

BRANDON: (*to REBECCA*) You're a smart person. I thought you might know.

ALEJANDRO: Will you guys please just calm down?

REBECCA: (to BRANDON) There are some things that an African-American person goes through and has…is born with…I don't know what the hell it is, but there is something there that a white person will never feel the same about. Same thing with a white person. But, I still am being oppressed. Minorities are still be oppressed. If I don't say anything, then who is going to know it is happening?

ANGIE: Come on, you guys. We're going to get in trouble again.

TEACHER: (*Once argument starts getting loud*) Keep it down. (*Pause.*) What did I just say? (*She tries to figure out what is going on*) Quiet! (*Pause.*) Quiet!! (*Everyone should finish talking except REBECCA*) Rebecca!!! Did I or did I not tell you we were on a tight schedule?!??! Get back to the project! Now!!

(*Pause*)

ANGIE: So, are we going to talk about Obama or not?

THE END

Developed by the *Giving Voice* Troupe, Spring of 2010 with the following actors in the roles:

BRANDON	***Drew Irwin***
REBECCA	***Kanome Jones***
ALEJANDRO	***Rolo Rodriguez***
ANGIE	***Samantha Long***
LENNON	***Dannie Patrick***
MALIK	***Ariel Forste***
TEACHER	***Chelsea Russell***

5 Character Development

Characters Are Key

"Oh, my gosh, I'm Logan! Honestly, I thought I was just being funny" (high school audience member realizing he acts like one of the main oppressors in a *Giving Voice* scenario). Once the script is established, it is time to work on the characters. A great deal of knowledge about the characters has naturally developed while workshopping the script. It is important to flesh out these characters beyond stereotypes. As in real life, be sure there are no perfect characters. There are three areas to be developed for each character: *Talking Points*, *Check In*, and *Backstory*. These may change slightly depending on the actor but there should be a consistency about what is important to share with the audience.

Talking Points

Talking Points make sure that certain voices are heard. These come from the issues to be addressed as illustrated by the scenario. The main goal of each actor during the *Talkback* phase of a forum is to have their character share certain information. If a character is not asked a direct question that allows the actor to share a *Talking Point*, then the actor must improvise a way to reveal that *Talking Point*.

Teacher or Leader. This type of character does not usually have many *Talking Points* since this is the character that the audience will replace in most instances. The following are possible *Talking Points* for the Teacher or Leader:

- I don't mean to "call out" the person of color, but they can be a leader if they are not so aggressive.
- I did not intend to offend anyone.
- I want students to have free discussions rather than be assigned a topic.
- I am not prepared to handle the situations and types of discussions that are happening.
- I want to do better but do not know how.
- I am afraid they will make the situation worse.
- I have very little or no diversity training.

DOI: 10.4324/9781032676883-5

- The only training required was an online multiple-choice test that could be retaken until passed. The training does nothing to help them handle the situations.

Characters of Color. Often for Characters of Color, there are numerous *Talking Points* that, unfortunately, have not changed over the years. The following are possible *Talking Points* for Characters of Color:

- It's hard to be the only one that looks like me in class.
- People who question my hair and touching it.
- I am often called on to speak for an entire race and I'm tired of being Black Google.
- I can no more speak for everyone who looks like me than a white person can speak for all white people.
  - People assume that I am from another country.
- People compliment me for speaking well.
- Others question if I deserve to be in college or if am I meeting a quota.
- People assume I have an athletic scholarship, not an academic scholarship.
- I'm afraid of standing up for myself because it often leads to being called aggressive.
- I am always followed in stores.
- Teachers call me out more than others, even when not doing anything, for instance, saying I wasn't paying attention when I was the only one taking notes.
- Last time I tried to talk to a teacher about something inappropriate, my assignments started going missing and my grade suffered.
- I have been stopped by police and feared for my life.

Additionally, biracial characters often need to address unique challenges such as the following:

- I have been told if I am part black then I am all black, like my other race does not exist.
- I especially hate when I fill out forms, like for scholarships, and I have to check just one box under ethnicity. Am I supposed to forget about my father or my mother?
- I deal with prejudice from both sides, even within my own family.

LGBTQ+. Again, there are numerous *Talking Points* that, unfortunately, have not changed much over the years. The following are possible *Talking Points* for LGBTQ+:

- I don't feel safe in a classroom, the halls, on campus, and so on.
- I have been told a church can help me which tells me I need to be fixed, like the whole "hate the sin, love the sinner." That is not in the Bible and all I hear is the "hate" part.
- Besides, I go to a very accepting church.

- When I am called a derogatory name, it is often an indication of violence.
- I feel attacked by politicians and others who do not know, much less understand, anyone in the LGBTQ+ community.
- I have thoughts of suicide. It can all be too much.
- I am afraid to come out to my parents or others. Sometimes this character is friends with another character who knows their sexual orientation.

Main Oppressor. While a straight white male is usually depicted as the main oppressor this should not be the only character that negatively contributes to the situation. The main oppressor should also have positive aspects that are revealed, often to the surprise of the audience that has made assumptions. The following are possible *Talking Points* for the main oppressor:

- I'm just joking.
- Everyone is too sensitive.
- There's a double standard such as a multi-cultural student union but no white student union.
- They already get the scholarships and jobs.
- Being gay is against religion. It is a choice.
- What's really wrong with the confederate flag? It's about heritage.

White Character. This character can share the frustration of wanting to do better but not knowing the best way to go about it. Also, there can be some dispelling of assumptions and opening the door for needed conversation. The following are possible *Talking Points* for the white character:

- I'm from a small town where everyone looks like me.
- Coming from a small town doesn't mean I'm stupid or fly the confederate flag.
- I want to do better, but I seem to say the wrong things.
- I just think my church can help, said to the LGBTQ+ Character. You know, "hate the sin, love the sinner."
- I don't see color.
- I don't understand what is wrong with believing all lives matter.
- My uncle is a police officer who does not do the awful things some do. I want him to come home safely too.

Other Examples.

- I didn't really like that candidate, but I voted for them anyway because being pro-life is important to me.
- I am from Columbia, Missouri, regarding the assumption that the individual is from the Columbia, the country, due to skin color.
- It's not "blacks." It's "Black people."
- If I fully stand up for myself, as anyone else would, I'm dismissed as just another "angry Black woman." I have even been called "uppity."

- Saying I am smart because I am Asian may seem like a compliment, but it is still a stereotype and harmful to those feeling the pressure, especially if they do not feel they live up to it.
- There has been an increase in hate crimes, especially because of the rhetoric being used, so, yes, I am afraid.

Time Out

The *Talking Points* are shared mostly in response to questions from the audience during the *Talkback* phase. Other characters can hear the responses and, if appropriate, respond to the other character. This lends even more realism but be careful, so the actors do not get caught up in arguing back and forth rather than moving on. However, there are things we think but do not share depending on who is around. This is what determines if a character takes a *Time Out* to share something with the audience that they do not want the other characters to hear. The other characters should engage in subtle activities such as writing on paper, reading, or looking at their phone, and avoid drawing attention from the character speaking during the *Time Out*.

The previous examples contain some possible moments for *Time Out*. The following are other possibilities:

Teacher or Leader. The main emphasis is this person does not know how to handle these situations, even though they want to address what is happening. Sometimes, this character refers to taking a generic online training that could be repeated until passed.

- I have not had training for these situations and don't know what to do.
- I think sometimes it is better to ignore these things because saying something can just make it worse.

Characters of Color. Often this character explains how exhausting it is to have to constantly educate others on what should be common respect or what they can look up themselves.

- Of course, it is prejudicial when teachers call me out without reason or call on me to speak for an entire community.
- I am afraid speaking up will make things worse.

LGBTQ+ Character. This character can address stereotypes, cruelty, and outing behaviors, even by those who say they are an ally.

- I do not feel safe.
- I am not sure which is worse: when the teacher does not address what others are saying or when they address it by bringing more attention to me. Sometimes, I am afraid to leave the classroom if the teacher brought the attention to me.
- My friend is the only one I trust to tell them my orientation, not these others.

- I don't feel safe to be my true self with the others or even the teacher, especially since some have made an assumption about who I am and have said hurtful things.
- I came out to my parents and was kicked out of the home. I was in a shelter for a while. Now I am staying with my aunt.
- Just a joke? Do you realize the suicide rates of LGBTQ+ students?
- I try not to call too much attention to myself because of what might happen.
- Relates a personal incident of bullying, being called a derogatory name, etc.

Main Oppressor. This is the chance to get the audience beyond the stereotype of privileged white male or female. Be cautious if an audience grasps onto feeling sorry for his situation, excusing his behavior, and stops addressing his oppressive behavior.

- I have a little brother who is on the spectrum and gets called the R-word (retarded). I don't like it when people use the word "retarded" in any context. My mom's boyfriend uses that word toward my brother. It's wrong.
- No, I don't see the irony. When I say things, it is to be funny, or it is the truth. My little brother was born like that, but that person chooses to be gay.

White Character. Audiences often overlook or possibly relate to this character and may not point out their oppressive behavior, even from ignorance.

- I have grown up around a family that has attitudes and says things I know are bad but what can I do?
- I actually have an uncle who is in the KKK. I am trying hard to not be like that. I'm learning.

There are many others *Talking Points* possible, depending on what is happening in the environment of the audience and, at times, the world. What the troupe chooses to address will depend on the actors available and the priority issues. Establishing the main *Talking Points* will help to build the full backstory for the characters and inform the stories that can be shared.

Check In

Using a *check in* following the scenario in phase one can help the actors, through their characters, to make the audience aware of particular struggles that should be addressed during the *Talkback* in phase two. Once the scenario ends, the facilitator can ask the characters to please give their character's name and *check in* by sharing how they are feeling or what they want the audience to know. These *check ins* should be a brief sentence or possibly only a word. The following are some examples:

Teacher or Leader. I'm frustrated and want them to have open discussions, calmly exchanging ideas without me stepping in to decide the topic for them.

Characters of Color. I am tired of being Black Google (or Latinx, Asian, etc.).

LGBTQ+. I don't want to be here (pause) at all. (Sometimes this character admits they are scared. This should be of special concern for the audience since it may indicate suicidal thoughts.)

Main Oppressor. I'm fine. Everyone is too sensitive.

White Character. I'm tired of being talked over and ignored or being attacked for my beliefs.

Intervention Needs

Each actor should have a main idea of what their character needs from those audience volunteers who intervene by trying an idea to help the situation. Knowing what their character needs will serve as their guiding principle. It will help inform their *Talking Points* and the feedback they give to the audience volunteers who participate in the *Intervention* phase. Here are some examples of what each character might need:

Teacher or Leader: None needed since the audience volunteer will intervene as this character.

Characters of Color:

- Someone to ask similar questions of all students, such as their thoughts on cultural awareness.
- Someone to pronounce their name correctly.

LGBTQ+:

- Someone to address the attacks without putting them on the spot, such as the teacher who states they are offended rather than the student being insulted is offended.
- Someone to respect their pronouns.
- Someone to use their chosen name.

Main Oppressor:

- Someone who won't make me feel attacked or like I am some awful human being.

White Character:

- Someone who will make me feel heard and will acknowledge my contributions

Backstories

There are usual questions during the *Talkback* in phase two but sometimes audiences will ask more personal questions trying to understand the characters better. These can include family situations, religion, politics, and many more. While the actors cannot cover everything, having a basic backstory can help them improvise answers. Of course, if the audience is getting too caught up in backstories, they are avoiding the main challenges of the scenario, and the facilitator should bring them back to the issues.

Backstories should include a variety of situations, some typical and a few that go against assumptions. Characters should know information such as how many are in their family, their status (birth order, only son, youngest, etc.), their responsibilities, and general home life. Not everyone has a mother and father in their home. This can become very interesting, especially if an audience member or another character asks about a "normal" family. Some characters might be working to help support their family. Not everyone goes to church or believes in some type of religion. If the scenario is set in college, then the characters are from different geographical areas and have different majors. If the setting is high school, there can still be students who have just moved there. Questions can come up about what their plans are after high school. This can include their majors, not necessarily knowing what they want their major to be, or even when college is not for everyone. Troupe members should integrate their work into a full character biography. This biography can be written by one or more actors working together who portray the same character. Adjustments can be made depending on the troupe members' own backstories (see Appendices G–K).

Cops in the Head Exercise

Once the backstories are well developed, there is an excellent but very challenging variation of a Boal exercise to enhance these characters called *Cops in the Head* (Boal, 1995). It is essential to ensure that a safe environment has been established and that someone trained for this type of exercise closely facilitates the exercise. *Cops in the Head* is a specific exercise amongst Boal's therapeutic techniques. It is a technique used to address internalized oppressions. Basically, the characters have "cops in their heads" or fears that have persisted after the oppressor no longer has "real" power over them. The following exercise is a modified variation for the purpose of enhancing the characters that have been developed for the scenario.

Decide the "Cops" for Each Character. Begin with discussions using the whole troupe or only the actors that play the same character. The following example is from a Black female character:

- I am most upset in the scenario when:
    - The Logan character does his version of ghetto slang.

- Identify three of the "cops" that influenced or continue to influence the character and what they said.
    - Biological father: "You are nothing but a stupid ho."
    - Teacher: "You'll never go to college because you can't play sports."
    - Rapper: Use rap lyrics of choice that depict the songs the character heard while growing up that demean women in horrible ways.

The Voices.

COP 1:

- Actor 1 (Black female actor in this example) takes a seated physical position or image to represent the moment in the scenario when their character is most upset.
- FREEZE.
- Actor 1 selects Actor 2 to take their place as the frozen image.
- Actor 2 takes Actor 1's place while Actor 1 becomes one of the identified *Cops in the Head* and a voice of why the character feels so upset.
- Actor 1 then repeatably says the words Cop 1 uses (slight movement may be used).
- Actor 1 then trades places with Actor 2 who becomes Cop 1 in the same manner demonstrated by Actor 1.
- With Actor 1 in the seated position again, they hear the voice of Cop 1 played by Actor 2 who repeats the words for their "cop in the head" until stopped by the facilitator. This usually lasts a very short time. Possibly repeat the words four to five times.

COP 2: This process is repeated until all three cops are established. Be sure to check in with the actors, especially Actor 1, and make sure they are ready to continue before moving to next cop.

- Actor 1 returns to their frozen image to represent the moment in the scenario when their character is most upset.
- Actor 1 selects Actor 3 to take their place as the frozen image.
- Actor 3 takes Actor 1's place while Actor 1 becomes a different identified "cop in the head" and another voice of why the character feels so upset.
- Actor 1 then says the words Cop 2 uses (some movement may be used).
- Actor 1 then trades places with Actor 3 who becomes Cop 2 in the same manner demonstrated by Actor 1.
- Actor 1 returns to the seated position again and hears the voices of Cop 1 and Cop 2 who repeat the words for their "cop in the head" until stopped by the facilitator. They can grow in intensity by repeating, overlapping, getting louder, and moving around Actor 1.

COP 3: Be sure to check in with the actors, especially Actor 1, and make sure they are ready to continue before moving to the final cop.

- Actor 1 returns to their frozen image to represent the moment in the scenario when their character is most upset.
- Actor 1 selects Actor 4 to take their place as the frozen image.
- Actor 4 takes Actor 1's place while Actor 1 becomes a different identified "cop in the head" and another voice of why the character feels so upset.
- Actor 1 then says the words Cop 3 uses (some movement may be used).
- Actor 1 then trades places with Actor 4 who becomes Cop 3 in the same manner demonstrated by Actor 1
- Actor 1 returns to the seated position again and hears the voices of Cop 1, Cop 2, and Cop 3 who repeat the words for their "cop in the head" until stopped by the facilitator. Again, the cops should grow in intensity by repeating, overlapping, getting louder, and moving around Actor 1.

Check in and Debrief

At this point, the exercise can get very intense, and the actors should be monitored closely and stopped early if necessary. Be sure there is positive reinforcement after finishing the exercise. Depending on what is acceptable by the troupe members this can include affirmative words for Actor 1 from the rest of the troupe or a big group hug! Be sure to debrief this exercise. It is important to check on the mental and emotional well-being of Actor 1. Are they truly, okay? Did this bring up something they want to share, either about themselves or the character? While most important for Actor 1, there should be some follow-up with the other actors who took on the negative voices, and what the other troupe members who observed felt. While there are various ways to modify *Cops in the Head*, one very effective addition is to have troupe members who are observing to take the place of Actor 1 to gain insights into that character and those represented. Additional modifications can be made depending on the troupe. This is a rare exercise used once for the final establishment of a character, but only with a trusting ensemble.

Characters Are Like People

Just like in real life, there are no perfect characters in the scenario. No one is completely good or bad. For instance, a character who tries to be politically correct uses a single word as an insult that is often overlooked as part of our current language. The character recognized as the white male oppressor does not feel privileged and works hard to afford college and support his single mom and little brother. Sometimes it has been assumed that dialogue has been created for the theatrical effect when it has been used verbatim from interviews. Alas, we can never top the true stories of what is said and done to some people in classrooms and across campuses.

Reference

Boal, A. (1995). *The rainbow of desire* (A. Jackson, Trans.). Routledge.

Appendix G

Bio by ________ Giving Voice Scenario: ________ Character: ________

Character Name: ________________

Backstory

Check-in

Talking Points

Time Out

What I have to say:

What I need to make the situation better?

Cops in the Head

I am most upset in the scenario when:

I am upset because of the following voices I have heard:
[This could be a friend, bully, parent, teacher, institution (church, media, rapper, etc.)]

Words of wisdom for other actors portraying this character

Appendix H

Bio by *Aerrionna* **Giving Voice Scenario:** *American History-Ferguson*

Character: *Chris*

Character Name: Chris Jones

Backstory

I am from Columbia, MO. I went (go) to high school with Riley. I moved around (due to military or?? ?) a lot growing up, so I've been exposed to many different cultures.

I am a sophomore at _______________University (or senior in high school) and I am (plan) majoring in English, I'd love to be a writer someday.

I grew up with two moms but have no siblings. My mom works for the VA and my mother is now a professor. My parents met in college.

Check-in

- **I'm so tired of being expected to answer for all black people. It's exhausting. I'm not "black Google."**

Talking Points

What I have to say:

- I'm not an experiment for my peers at school.
- I should be able to identify my race as both a black person and as a biracial person.
- BLM is not a hate group but a response to hate. I am tired of being scared. [Talk about handling police and racists (remarks/actions)]
- I am losing my faith. How many times am I to forgive hatred?
    - Actually, I am not a Baptist. I am a _______________ (after assumption made)

- Privilege is scariest when someone doesn't realize they have it.
- Taking a knee is no more opposing the flag than Rosa Parks was opposing bus transportation.

What I need to make the situation better:

- Need to not be used for the sake of the project.
- Fellow students must be held accountable by an authority figure for slights against me.
- People to get to know me based on merit and interests, not race.
- A safe space to be who I am.

Time Out

- I want to defend Riley (gay character) but they do not want attention brought to themselves. I do not want to make things worse.

Cops in the Head

I am most upset in the scenario when: Angie talks about "When I see a thug listening to rap music with a hoodie"

I am upset because of the following voices I have heard:

[This could be a friend, bully, parent, teacher, institution (church, media, rapper, etc.)]

People trying to determine race: What are you?
Black friends: You don't act like a *real* black person.
White people: If you listen to police, you'll be fine.

Words of wisdom for other actors portraying this character

Chris is not allowed to out Riley. Says the R-word out of frustration. Doesn't want their race to be the center of attention. "Breaks" down a bit as talk about being only one in classes, people avoiding them, followed in stores, being stopped by police for no reason, having their white friends asked if they are okay by police who stopped Chris…

Appendix I

Bio by *Corey* **Giving Voice Scenario:** *American History*

Character: *Logan*

Character Name: Logan Todd

Backstory

- From a rough neighborhood.
- Lower middle-class, socio-economics.
- Works evening to try and help out with the family.
- Single mom and younger brother, brother is on the Autism Spectrum but is higher functioning.
- Mom's boyfriend uses R-Word in general and to brother.
- Raised Catholic but is no longer practicing at all.

Check-in

- **Everyone is just too sensitive**

Talking Points

What I have to say:

- If needed (or when "attacked" by audience) Points out no one has called out Chris for R-word.
- Culture is fine but no one asks me about mine or how unprivileged I am.
- What is this white privilege? I'm going to school and working to try to afford college, Blacks are basically guaranteed scholarships but not for me?
- Joking is just who I am.
- Tired of being blamed for everything: didn't own slaves, didn't keep women from voting.
- Taking a knee disrespects the flag and what soldiers have fought for. Isn't football or celebrity's place. That's not how you protest.
- Police brutality happens to criminals – some are white
- Isn't calling a guy a "dick" the same thing?

What I need to make the situation better?

- I need people to actually get to know me, instead of labeling me as a problem or dismissing me as a lost cause.
- People need to have a sense of humor, and not take everything so seriously.

Cops in the Head

I am most upset in the scenario when:

- Chris uses the R-word.

I am upset because of the following voices I have heard:

[This could be a friend, bully, parent, teacher, institution (church, media, rapper, etc.)]

- Mom's boyfriend uses the R-word to my own brother.
- Black Lives Matter says to me that my life does not matter.
- Teachers dismissing me as a problem student or a racist.

Words of wisdom for other actors portraying this character

Do not lose your humanity. Be a real person. There is a lot of good in you. You really are just joking. It is fine around your friends and family.

Appendix J

Bio by *Samantha* **Giving Voice Scenario:** *American History*

Character: *Angie*

Character Name: Angie Bryant

Backstory

I'm from Cole Camp, MO, a small farming community. People literally drive tractors to school. My family is very Catholic and I'm the oldest of 3 children. My parents are married, my Mom is a teacher and my Dad is a lineman for a power company. I want to go to college for nursing/I'm a nursing major (if in college). I just moved to this school three weeks ago and I feel out of place. I don't really know anyone and I'm having trouble making friends. I'm very connected to my Catholic faith, but I don't really discuss it with others, but I secretly judge others based on my religious beliefs (coming from a good, loving place). I have a problem with people who are gay, abortion, profanity and pre-marital sex.

Check-in

- **I'm tired of being treated like I am ignorant just because I come from a small town. I just want to get this done.**

Talking Points

What I have to say:

1. I need a scholarship, or need to maintain it in order to go to/stay in College. Nobody in class will stay on topic or focus on our assignment. I get very frustrated with this class. I just want a good grade.
2. I think discussing race/touchy subjects is important, but the classroom is NOT the place for it. I come from a place where "Everyone looks like me" so I'm not used to all this fighting and diversity in the classroom.

3. I just want to get the work DONE!

   If asked: The "Muslims" outside the door really did freak me out.

   If asked: The teacher's story was just trying to relate to the students and I didn't think it was offensive or racist. I did notice some of my classmates seemed uncomfortable though, but I'm not sure why.

What I need to make the situation better?

I need structure from the leader, set rules, and a presence from the teacher to keep class focused and on topic. (Be able to pick our own groups.) Sometimes this is a joke Angie likes to make.

Cops in the Head

I am most upset in the scenario when: Rebecca says, "Oh you poor thing, you must have been oppressed all your life."

I am upset because of the following voices I have heard:

[This could be a friend, bully, parent, teacher, institution (church, media, rapper, etc.)]

Parents: You have to get good grades and scholarships because we can't afford to send you to a university.

Catholic Church: Catholic views through and through. These teachings are cemented in her mind.

Words of wisdom for other actors portraying this character

Be careful not to judge Angie. She means well and really does want to understand other cultures and people. She's just ignorant of a lot of things. But don't forget she's a real person and someone has to represent her too!

Appendix K

Bio by *Kanome* **Giving Voice Scenario:** *American History*
Character: *Rebecca*

Character Name: Rebecca McDonald

Backstory

- I was born originally in Tacoma, WA; I moved to Little Rock, AR ten years ago
    - Little Rock, AR is where my mother's family is from
- I have two younger siblings, 16 and 12 and an older brother, 25
- I attended (*insert university*) because I wanted to stay in close proximity to home but not so close that my mother would come and visit
    - I want my family to visit, but not too often, I am here to gain an education and discover more about myself as an individual
- My mother is a large influence on me – As a single parent, there was a lot she had to do and put up with, merely because she was a black woman
    - She would just let people talk about her and, then come back and told me what she would have said. I understand why she never said anything the job and the money were more important at the time
    - She made me promise to make my voice and my opinions heard because, regardless of what anyone says, they are important.
    - Actually she said, "Don't let anyone ever shut you up." – I've modified that a bit because there are circumstances where it is not appropriate to voice my opinion
- I am currently a junior majoring in Journalism – I am more interested in print journalism because I love writing articles and editorials; if I did broadcast, it would be more field work, not a consistent anchor
    - I know that everyone can get a newspaper online now but I still feel that there is a good number of people that like the paper with their morning coffee and not their computer

- I am an honors student with a 3.9 cumulative grade point average
- I am going to apply for graduate school at New York University for their Journalism program – I don't quite know my emphasis yet, maybe international relations, cultural reporting, or news and documentaries
- In order to prepare for this, I write small articles for the Springfield News-Leader, just small articles and some of my faculty members have told me that if I wrote something, they would look at it and give me pointers
- I consider myself to be a very respectful person; I become very passionate about the affairs concerning African-Americans and white people because we are the historically disadvantaged group and there are some individuals that still believe that it is okay to treat African Americans as such – or worse, to treat every African American within the confines of the stereotypes that persists.
- I try very hard to search for the truth and advocate for the variety that exists with the African American culture and not allow myself to be labeled or put into a box. I am very proud of my culture and there are differences to celebrate.
- I am interested in making everyone aware of these differences so that they can appreciate them as well as educate others about the world, so we can have an informed dialogue about affairs of race and politics and other topics

Check-in

- **I'm so tired of people talking to me as some type of "every Black person."**

Talking Points

What I have to say:

- I have to let everyone know why I am passionate when I feel that I am being stereotyped.
    - I know that stereotypes result out of truth but individuals have to know that it is not correct to make those assumptions. I've been stereotyped all my life because of the way I talk or carry myself and I don't like to be placed in a category merely because that person doesn't want to take the time to get to know me. So I make sure to address the issue if I can.
- I also have to address why I don't say anything when the instructor addresses me in a heightened tone.
    - Although, I do feel slightly persecuted by the professor and some of the things that she might say, I am a respecter of authority. I want a

job when I graduate, so not only do I need good grades, but I will need instructors to write recommendation letters. There was an incident with another instructor when I, respectfully and privately pointed out something he said that was offensive. My papers started going missing.
  - I feel that I can speak up and educate my peers though

- I try to be politically correct. I have to say that I don't think I'm right all the time or just want to cause conflict – I grew up in an environment where I wasn't allowed to voice my opinions or because of my skin color, my opinions didn't count.

  - I want to help others gain knowledge yet I also want to learn more from others.
  - I don't think that I know everything but if someone asks me a question or poses an opposition, I will let the person know what I think. And if I'm wrong, I would like to know why, so that I can take that information and hopefully share it with someone else who might have thought the same way I did.

What do I need to make the situation better?

- I need for the instructor to moderate the group discussion so that we can focus on our topic.
- I need the instructor say something when politically incorrect statements or actions happen.
- I need an apology from Brandon and for him and others not act with ignorance and make those assumptions.

Cops in the Head

I am most upset in the scenario when: Brandon does his ghetto slang

I am upset because of the following voices I have heard:

[This could be a friend, bully, parent, teacher, institution (church, media, rapper, etc.)]

My biological father: "You are nothing but a stupid black hoe. You'll never go to college cause you can't play sports."

I grew up hearing songs demeaning women in horrible ways. (insert lyrics of choice)

College Recruiter: "you don't sound black."

6 Forum Facilitation

Facilitator or Joker

"We are all *actors*: being a *citizen* is not living in society, it is changing it" (Boal, 2009, p. 2). The facilitator is key to guiding audience members to become spect-actors, in order to change the scene for the better. In Boal's Forum Theatre, the term Joker is used for what many would call the facilitator. While many practitioners or guides of *Theatre of the Oppressed* are referred to as Jokers, Boal insisted the Joker has very little power and does not decide anything. Often the Joker is explained using a deck of cards where the Joker does not belong to any one suit. It does not take sides. Boal believed effectiveness of a *Theatre of the Oppressed* forum diminishes with the extent the Joker imposes their viewpoint on various situations or interventions.

Using the term facilitator is easier for others to understand and gives a freedom to step in with guidance or knowledge if necessary. However, it is still best to limit the interference of the facilitator in the actual discussions that happen. After the facilitator explains what to expect in the forum and readies the audience, they should fade from the scenario and characters except to coordinate the check in, questions, and interventions. If the facilitator is constantly telling the audience why something should or should not be said or done, then it becomes a lecture similar to most diversity training. Moreover, the words and emotions of the characters provide much more powerful interactions with the audience and are often more lasting.

Another important aspect of guiding the troupe and being the facilitator of a forum is an awareness of how each troupe member is doing during and after a forum. Some characters can definitely take a toll on an actor, especially if they are not able to keep themselves separate. The most obvious are the characters that are targeted by several microaggressions. Even with a trusting ensemble, there are times that something said or done may affect an actor more than usual. It could be something in the script performed many times or an interaction with an audience member during *Talkbacks* or *Intervention*. As

DOI: 10.4324/9781032676883-6

the facilitator, be ready to step in, if needed, or if communicated by the actor. Always check in with everyone after a forum, even if you think everything went well. Even as the facilitator, you can miss a small moment that has affected an actor deeply.

Preparing the Audience

After introducing themselves and the troupe in general, the facilitator should welcome the audience and assure them it is their safe environment for the purpose of the forum. This is important for the audience to know so they are more open to participation, even with difficult subjects for them.

Let the audience know the goals of the forum. This should include an understanding of microaggressions or bullying. Another goal is to give voice to those who feel they cannot speak up for themselves or who are not being heard. An additional goal is for the audience to become more aware of and to recognize oppression. Finally, the ultimate goal is for the audience to take action to address the oppression happening to others, thus creating their own safe environment.

Next, the facilitator should explain how the scenario they are about to see was developed. This should emphasize the true personal narratives that were gathered and workshopped into the script and used for the forum. The audience will hear and see the oppression some people go through.

The facilitator next prepares the audience for the three phases of the forum by explaining each phase:

Phase I is the *Scenario* and includes a warmup and the scenario developed by the troupe to be used for the purpose of the forum.

Phase II is the *Talkback* where the audience gets to ask the characters questions and gain insights to use in the final phase.

Phase III is *Intervention* when the scenario is performed again only this time the audience can stop the oppression, enter the scenario, and try an idea to improve the situation.

The audience is now ready to begin Phase I with a warmup. Naturally, each facilitator should develop their own style of facilitation and adjust the introduction for audience and time. A sample facilitator script is included (see Appendix L).

Reference

Boal, A. (2009, March 25). *Message of Augusto Boal*. World Theatre Day. https://world-theatre-day.org/pdfs/WTD_Boal_2009.pdf

Appendix L

Introduction

On behalf of Missouri State University's *Giving Voice* troupe, welcome to your safe environment. This is important to remember as we deal with situations that are not always comfortable and often result in Difficult Dialogues, or as we like to call them, Courageous Conversations, as we look for meaningful ways to improve our wonderfully diverse world of ours. We also like to say we take diversity training to a new level. We do that by providing the missing component that recent studies have identified for affective training – the opportunity to practice. *Giving Voice* strives to literally give voice to those who, for whatever reason feel they cannot speak up themselves. Our goal is for you to become more aware of oppression, especially microaggressions, those brief, subtle, and commonplace indignities: a comment, a joke, a word that has made it into our vernacular. Whether intentional or unintentional, they communicate insults and have been shown to have harmful psychological impacts. If we are not the target, we might not even notice but for those who endure these, day after day, it is like constant dripping water that can wear away even the toughest stone. Someone described it as death by a thousand tiny cuts. The most common tactic used to deal with oppression is to ignore it. However, know that silence indicates approval. We hope you will not only become more aware but be empowered to take action to improve your environment for everyone in your space: free from microaggressions, bullying, and other forms of oppression.

****

What you are about to see came from research on oppression happening in college classrooms. The troupe members and I conducted interviews of students and teachers and then used these true personal stories of oppression to develop the scenario you are about to see which is set in an American History class. We incorporated a lot of stories into this scenario; however, remember the issues and situations depicted are real, affecting people regularly in classrooms and beyond.

****

Explain the three phases

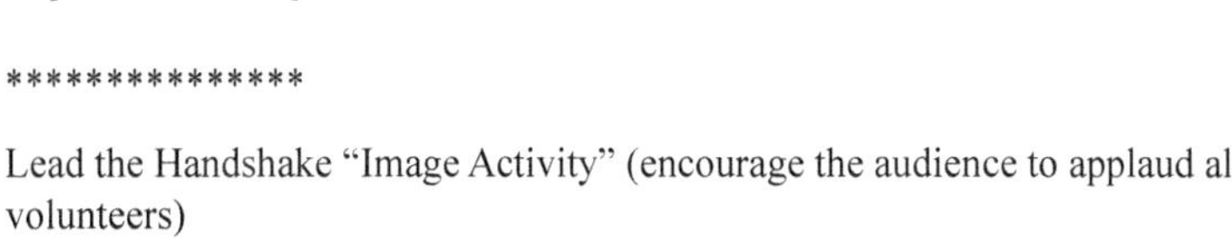

****

Lead the Handshake “Image Activity” (encourage the audience to applaud all volunteers)

****

1. SCENERIO

****

2. TALKBACK (remind the audience they are talking to characters and not the actors)

****

3. INTERVENTION (review the rules, including NO Magic or Mayhem)

Lead the Circle and Cross exercise

Begin the scenario again

APPLAUD all interveners, using their names, when they begin and when they end their intervention.

****

Possibly review oppressions not mentioned or did not have time to address
Have the actors introduce themselves

Encourage the audience to continue Courageous Conversations

7 Phase I

Scenario

Handshake Warmup

"Thou shalt not be a victim, thou shalt not be a perpetrator, but, above all, thou shalt not be a bystander" (Bauer, 2006, p.8). The final audience preparation before the scenario in Phase I is Boal's *Handshake* (Boal, 1992) exercise. It is intended to begin easing audience members from being spectators to becoming spect-actors. This exercise highlights subjective reactions to people we see. Ask for two people to volunteer to come to the front. It sometimes helps to let the audience know the volunteers will not have to say anything. Be sure to encourage applause for the volunteers. The facilitator should have them shake hands and call "freeze" at the moment they are shaking hands. Let them know the hard part for them will be to stay frozen.

Ask for someone in the audience to *objectively* describe the image. Few people will actually describe the image of the two people with true facts, thus objectively, such as *there are two people, one is taller than the other* or *one is wearing a blue shirt*. Instead, the most common descriptions will be subjective such as *they are shaking hands* or *she is nervous.* As soon as someone uses a subjective description, stop and point this out to the audience. Reassure them that most people would do the same. Then, encourage the audience to give only subjective descriptions. These may include *they are making a deal,* or *they are dancing.*

After a few subjective descriptions, allow one of the volunteers to return to their seat. Again, be sure to encourage applause for them. Ask the volunteer that is left to recreate their frozen image, only without the other person. Then ask the audience to again give subjective descriptions. Usually, you will get more descriptions such as *he is opening a door,* or *they are reaching for something.* Again, after a few descriptions, stop and allow the remaining volunteer to return to their seat, with applause.

Point out to the audience how much easier it was to come up with ideas when there was only one person. Help the audience to recognize that we rarely see the full picture of what is happening, who people really are, or what they are doing. Instead, we fill in the blanks by making assumptions. These

DOI: 10.4324/9781032676883-7

assumptions are based on our own backgrounds and experiences. Finally, guide the audience to look for assumptions in the scenario they are about to see. These can be assumptions the characters are making about each other or what audience members may be making about the characters. Then they can clarify these assumptions during the *Talkback* Phase, which will help them during the *Intervention* Phase.

Scenario

Remind the audience where the scenario is set, but that it could be anywhere people interact. Also, explain that there are a lot of microaggressions demonstrated in the one scenario for the purpose of the forum, but these happen regularly in classrooms and beyond. This first phase concludes with the actual scenario presented as conventional theatre. The audience watches a short play.

References

Bauer, Y. (2006, January 27). IHRD Yehuda Bauers speech.doc. https://www.holocaustremembrance.com/press-room/speeches

Boal, A. (1992). *Games for actors and non-actors* (A. Jackson, Trans.). Routledge.

8 Phase II

Talkback

Check In

"I loved just talking with the characters even though I realized I say some of those things. I never thought of it being hurtful. The impact really is more important than the intent" (*Giving Voice* Forum audience member). Phase II begins with the *Check In.* After the scenario ends, the facilitator acknowledges the characters may have gone through a rough time and would like for each one to introduce themselves and *Check In.* It is best to start with the teacher or leader and end with the "white oppressor" stating something like, "I'm fine. Everyone is just too sensitive." Remember this is an opportunity to not only remind the audience of names but, more importantly, to allow the characters to say something that can help guide the audience's initial questions.

The facilitator reminds the audience that they will be interacting with the characters in a safe environment. Again, let the audience know this is a unique opportunity to ask certain questions and interact with those that they would not necessarily feel comfortable. The facilitator can give some example questions to help get the audience started, if needed.

Talkback

Prompt the audience to ask questions that will help them determine interventions that would help the situation. Be prepared to steer some audience members away from lecturing the characters about their behavior. Instead, turn this into an opportunity to remind the audience members about Phase III: *Intervention* when they will have the opportunity to try ways to help. Until then, encourage the audience to ask questions to get to know the characters better and learn what the characters need to improve the situation for the characters. Be careful of actors that may want to react angrily depending on the phrasing of questions. Train actors if the audience is negative to not to reciprocate in the same manner but rather show the harm that does to the character. Actors that allow themselves to portray anger will only shut down the audience. Finally, remind

DOI: 10.4324/9781032676883-8

the audience that the actors will remain in character until the end of the forum. At that time, the actors will introduce themselves. Until then, they will answer and interact as the character with the character's background, experience, feelings, etc. Now you are ready for the *Check In* using what was developed for each character.

The facilitator now asks for questions. Repeating the question is helpful in case other audience members do not hear it clearly. If it is a large audience, have helpers with portable microphones go to those with questions so that everyone can hear the questions.

During this phase, the audience interacts directly with the characters. The actors stay in character while answering questions from the audience. This is where the extensive background developed during the rehearsal process is utilized. Each actor is ready to answer questions from family backgrounds, why they did or said something during the scenario, or how something that was said or done made them feel. This is when the audience has the opportunity to engage in courageous conversations in a safe environment. During this phase, the audience has the chance to ask questions many would not feel comfortable asking outside this environment, especially of people who are different from them. All characters are a part of this phase and may react to answers other characters give.

Also, characters may call a *Time Out* to answer a particularly sensitive question. When a *Time Out* is initially used, the facilitator should explain that only the audience and not the other characters can hear what is being said. Remind the audience that we do not always say out loud what we are thinking, depending on who can hear. *Time Outs* are used when a character wants to answer without the other characters hearing them, in order to reveal more about their situation or past they are not comfortable with others knowing. This is often done out of fear of repercussions or something very personal that has happened to them. A *Time Out* may be used to reveal something about the character that they do not want the other characters to know. It could be used to reveal how badly they feel because there is something in their background that makes the situation more difficult. One character in the *American History* scenario uses the *Time Out* to reveal sexual orientation to the audience. Another example is a character that calls *Time Out* might need to share with the audience that they are a survivor of sexual assault. Moreover, they were triggered by another character who casually complained about doing badly on a test by saying, "I just got raped by my Biology test!"

The audience uses the *Talkback* Phase to get to know the characters better, clear up assumptions, and find out how the situation can be improved for each individual character. Audience members then use the knowledge acquired during this phase to form ideas to try to improve the situation during the final Phase III: *Intervention*.

9 Phase III

Intervention

Practice

"In the end, we will remember not the words of our enemies, but the silence of our friends" (King, n.d.). The *Intervention* Phase of a *Giving Voice* forum is the key to successful diversity training. Studies have identified a missing key component in conventional diversity training: the need to practice what is learned. Attaining the confidence to act rather than ignore oppression is established by practice outside of the classroom. The *Intervention* Phase of the forum meets this newly recognized need for faculty and others to practice, in order to attain comfort in addressing issues of microaggressions (Sue, 2010). Ideally, in a full-length forum, the audience has time to brainstorm ideas for the teacher or leader on how to intervene in the various situations that come up during the scenario.

After the *Talkback*, the actors will reset the scenario in order to perform the scenario again. Sometimes, it is helpful to remind the actors to reset themselves by "shaking off" any negativity from Phase I or II. They are to start new as if it is the first time happening. The facilitator explains the rules for the *Intervention* Phase.

Rules

The facilitator should explain the audience will witness the same scenario; only this time, they can stop the oppression. At any point during the replaying of the scenario, audience members may raise their hand and say "stop" in order to address an act of oppression. The person who stopped the scenario may volunteer to join the scenario and try an idea to address the oppression. If they are reluctant, someone else can volunteer. The facilitator should work diligently to get the first volunteer, as this will open the door for others to follow suit.

Reluctance is the main reason not to use a stage in a theatre. Going "on stage" will add to the challenge of audience members volunteering. Ideally, the audience will be able to join the scenario easily.

DOI: 10.4324/9781032676883-9

No Magic – No Mayhem

The facilitator should explain the rules of *no magic* and *no mayhem. Magic* is saying or doing something unrealistic. *Magic* might be stopping the oppression before it happens, basically because they have seen the scenario already and know to tell a character not to say what they are about to say. The audience may call it "*magic*" or it can be pointed out by the facilitator. The objective of the *Intervention* Phase is to let the oppression happen and intervene with an idea to improve the situation. Remind the audience that despite best efforts, oppression happens. No *mayhem* basically means no physical confrontation.

Warmup: Circle and Cross

Before beginning the *Intervention* Phase, the facilitator leads the audience in the *Circle and Cross* activity (Boal, 1992). This is a fun way to focus the audience for the *Intervention* Phase. Ask the audience to draw a circle in the air with their right index finger. Demonstrate this with them for a few moments. Then, ask the audience to make a cross, or plus sign, in the air with their left index finger. Again, demonstrate this with them for a few moments. Now, ask the audience to do both at the same time. Allow them to try for a few moments, since this usually brings some laughter.

Finally, ask them if they could earn a $1,000, or some other applicable reward, if they could do both at the same time, would they be able to do it? Most will admit that yes, with practice, they could. This is a fun way to talk with the audience about how difficult the exercise is now, but how they could teach themselves to do both at the same time, with practice. This is when you point out the *Intervention* Phase is their chance to practice. This is not only a chance to practice, but to do so in a safe environment.

Volunteers

The volunteer asks the actors to "rewind" or "fast-forward" to a particular place in the scenario. The volunteer joins the scenario in the place of the teacher or leader. This is very effective, in the moment, training. It is a chance to try an idea on how to handle a situation rather than remain silent, as well as to try it in a safe environment.

The volunteer may stay in for as long as they wish. Most interventions are for a short time. The volunteer tries their idea and stops. They then return to their seat. Another unique aspect is the chance to get feedback on how their idea worked for the characters. More than one can volunteer to address the same oppression, or the scenario can continue until someone again says "stop."

Feedback

Feedback comes from the perspective of the characters themselves. The actors should be trained to give their response in first person as the character and from how the character feels the intervention worked, or did not work, for them. Be cautious of experienced actors who will want to tell the volunteer or audience how to intervene while forgetting to speak as the character. Just as in the *Talkback* Phase, be careful of actors that may want to react angrily to the intervention. If the audience is negative, train actors not to reciprocate in the same manner. This will only shut down the audience. The *feedback* reinforces the fact that there are no magic answers. The interveners should try to do the "most good" without shutting down characters. For instance, an intervener may tell the character who is talking about getting "raped by a biology test" how inappropriate that was, and to not add to the rape culture. Some characters may give *feedback*, thanking the intervener and talking about feeling safer. In contrast, the character using the phrase about being "raped by a biology test" might be upset and feel attacked. Depending on the technique, the character using that phrase might appreciate understanding how their choice of words could affect others.

Practice

The facilitator should remind the audience that silence indicates approval. In other words, if no one stops the oppression, they are indicating they are fine with the oppression. Furthermore, if no one changes things, then, as in real life, nothing will change. Begin the scenario again. Unlike other forms of diversity training, an individual can try ideas with the *Giving Voice* troupe and receive feedback before trying an idea for the first time in an actual situation. All interventions will help the audience learn what to do and sometimes, just as importantly, what not to do.

Intervention may be as simple as saying "Ow!" when one of the students calls another "retarded," and then calmly explaining why that is a hurtful word. Another intervention may be stating no tolerance for derogatory comments against a member of the LGBTQ+ community. This is done without drawing attention to the member of the LGBTQ+ community in the scenario who was the target of the oppression. Other interventions may require more elaborate best practices to improve the situation. Minimally, the forum starts the courageous conversations needed to shed light on the various oppressions and microaggressions that plague environments. With that awareness, we can begin to combat them. We hope the audience will not only become more aware but be empowered to take action to improve their own environment for all their students.

References

Boal, A. (1992). *Games for actors and non-actors* (A. Jackson, Trans.). Routledge.

King, M. L., Jr. Quotes. (n.d.). Amnestyusa.org. Retrieved December 7, 2023, from amnestyusa.org. Web site: https://www.amnestyusa.org/updates/15-powerful-martin-luther-king-jr-quotes/

Sue, D. (2010). *Microaggressions in everyday life: Race, gender, and sexual orientation*. John Wiley & Sons.

10 Title IX

Sexual Assault

"I believe you" (audience member to rape survivor character during a *Giving Voice Intervention*). After the debut of *Giving Voice* for the university's leadership team in May of 2010, there were numerous requests for forums within the university for the following academic year. This was followed by community organizations and businesses. However, a more important shift in our work came at the request of our provost to use *Giving Voice* to address Title IX issues and training.

The Obama administration had clarified college and university responsibilities for the prevention and response to sexual assault incidents on campus.[1] The document from the United States Department of Education Office for Civil Rights clearly outlined adjudication of sexual assault incidents as falling within the bounds of Title IX protections and requiring institutions to take action (Ali, 2011). Until this clarification, Title IX was best known for giving women equal opportunities in sports. Due to brave people speaking up and taking action, the emphasis shifted to Title IX's basic principle, the right to a safe educational environment, an environment free from bullying and harassment, including sexual harassment and sexual assault.

During the fall semester, while also holding forums, research on sexual harassment and sexual violence on our campus was conducted. At the time, more than one in five women on college campuses would be the victims of sexual assault or attempted sexual assault (National Sexual Violence Resource Center (NSVRC), 2015). One early takeaway when we began researching this was a preference for the terms sexual assault or sexual misconduct, when what was really being talked about was rape, which has nothing to do with sex. Rape is about violence, and it is not limited to women. The troupe members focused on students' experiences, including if they had shared these experiences with someone and, if reported, how it was handled. Other research focused on the support available from the university.

Once again, true personal narratives were shared by those who had experienced inappropriate comments in response to their experiences as survivors of

DOI: 10.4324/9781032676883-10

rape. We learned there was a need to help victims become survivors of sexual violence. We also became more aware that rape is not confined to women. For the research project for *Giving Voice* in the area of Title IX, we were asked to address the latest issues related to Title IX. The focus was on sexual assault and harassment with an emphasis on intervention and empowering audience members to be *upstanders* rather than *bystanders*. This particular topic did not lend itself to the usual singular scenario, so we developed several forums with audiences. Each scenario addressed, the all-too-common occurrences of sexual harassment and assault and included.

Club Scene

Often used in conjunction with *Juxtapose*, this scenario is set in a nightclub where three female friends arrive to have fun. One of the characters is the designated driver, but the other two characters have already started drinking before arriving at the club. A young man buys drinks for and tries to get one of the friends, who has had the most to drink, to leave her friends and go with him to a house party.

Social Media

The premise addresses the issues from a compromising picture of a female student that has gone viral on various forms of social media. The female character knows she did not drink very much. However, she does remember finishing a drink a young man gave her, but she does not remember the rest of the night.

Midterm

This scenario depicts questionable contact and discussions a male instructor has with a female student. It examines the power role of the male instructor over a freshman female not sure what is acceptable at the college level. The use of social media and inappropriate messaging is also addressed.

Juxtapose

The examination of one night's events turned out to be a powerful scenario for Title IX forums, especially for training those the victims chose to confide in about being sexually assaulted. The scenario reveals two perspectives on the events of a night of drinking. One is a young man telling his friend about matching with a girl on social media, getting together with the girl at a party, drinking, taking her to a friend's house so she would not get in trouble at her residence hall, and eventually having sex, even though she was reluctant at first. The female perspective is told to her friend about matching with the male, meeting at a party, drinking too much, being offered to stay at a house so she would not get into trouble, but later being forced to have sex. The friend even asks the victim if she is sure she was raped since she was "really drunk."

These forums follow the phases of a regular forum but not extensively. The *Talkback* Phase allows for questions of all characters, including the friends and their reaction to what they have heard. Questions included:

- Does the character believe his friend is a rapist?
- Will he report his friend or at least confront him?
- Why does a character sound like she is blaming her friend for what happened?

More importantly, key *Talking Points* allowed for sharing frustrations about prevalent double standards and misconceptions, such as the following character comments:

> Why are girls told what not to wear when they go to college and given pepper spray, but boys are told to have a good time and given condoms?
>
> I should be able to wear something sexy and feel good about myself without worrying about being raped.
>
> I could walk down the street naked and that still wouldn't mean I was asking for it.
>
> Everyone worries about HIS promising future but what about mine?
>
> I froze, no words would come out but silence is not consent.

Phase III of this particular forum only allows for intervention as one of the friends. This is especially good for someone, such as a friend or faculty, to learn or demonstrate a better response than what the character shows. One of the most important aspects is for the person to let the victim know they believe them. "I believe you" is a powerful and needed response. Therefore, if you are the person a victim confides in, your reaction will likely determine if they tell anyone else.

Considerations

The confidant's reaction often determines if the victim reports to an official who can clarify options available, such as steps to ensure safety, counseling, and investigation. As of this writing, according to The Criminal Justice System: Statistics at RAINN.org (2023), more than two out of three sexual assaults are not reported.

This is a chance to remind the confidant they do not investigate or decide if reporting is needed. They can reassure the victim of the support available. They can offer to go with the victim to report. Depending on the confidant, such as faculty, reporting is mandatory.

This particular forum also allows for clarification of university rules that students may not realize. Many universities do not contact parents or police without consent. Some university residence halls do not report drinking unless there is a medical issue. Other substance-related myths that are clarified include the fact that consent cannot be given if someone is alcohol or drug impaired. Moreover, alcohol or drug impairment is not an acceptable excuse for the rapist.

Facilitators should be prepared for a variety of responses. Be sure to warn the audience since the scenario and discussions may trigger some audience members. It is also recommended to have a counselor available. Also, be aware of the troupe members. No matter how determined, they too could be triggered. This can occur even if they helped develop the scenario and have performed in it. There is also the occasional comment or intervention from an audience member that may trigger something in a troupe member.

Note

1 The clarifications and requirements of the Obama administration were subsequently rescinded by the next administration.

References

Ali, R. (2011, April 4). *Dear Colleague Letter*. U.S. Department of Education. https://www2.ed.gov/print/about/offices/list/ocr/letters/colleague-201104.html

National Sexual Violence Resource Center. (2015). 2015: College Campuses. https://www.nsvrc.org/

The Criminal Justice System: Statistics. (2023, July 22). rainn.org. https://www.rainn.org/statistics/criminal-justice-system

11 Audience Impact

Audience Effectiveness

Theatre is the art of looking at ourselves (Boal, 1992). *Giving Voice* was originally developed to address microaggressions in a university setting. Microaggressions cut across all social identities including race, ethnicity, religion, nationality, sexual orientation, gender identity, gender expression, age, ableness, socio-economic class, religion, and other important social dimensions. These insults and invalidations occur throughout organizations, including all majors, departments, and colleges in a university.

Research shows that teachers' attitudes toward diversity have measurable impact on educational effectiveness. Even the most experienced teachers are ill-prepared to productively and successfully facilitate diversity discussions and interactions (Sue et al., 2009; Unruh & McCord, 2010)

Audience Safe Space

In the first few years of *Giving Voice* forums, surveys were used to evaluate its effectiveness with audiences. The first question explored the impact on participants experiencing *Giving Voice* for diversity professional development in higher education. The results showed an appreciation for a safe space to interact with the diverse characters in the scenario. Another impact reported by participants was the realization of a need to acknowledge and address microaggressions. The third most common finding was that the discussions the audience engaged in during the forum were rarely a lived reality. Often, audience members do not have the opportunity to have these discussions with people different from themselves. Unfortunately, if they do, most audience members are reluctant about approaching various subjects for fear of saying something wrong or appearing ignorant.

Audience Awareness

Another major question explored through the surveys of audience members was whether the participants increased their awareness of microaggressions.

DOI: 10.4324/9781032676883-11

Two main findings became clear with the results. The first result revealed an enhanced awareness of the multicultural dimensions of teaching. The second result showed a positive impact on recognizing and understanding microaggressions.

Audience Empowerment

The third area explored by the survey was the impact a *Giving Voice* forum has on empowering participants to address the issues of microaggressions in the classroom. This area is particularly important since the most common tactic used to address microaggressions is to ignore them. There were four main results for this part of the survey. Many participants reported feeling their cultural competencies had improved. Additionally, they reported being more confident to address issues of oppression they now more easily recognize. From a combination of *Talkback* discussions and interventions, a third empowering result included new and effective resources to confront diversity issues, including microaggressions. Finally, those who volunteered during the *Intervention* Phase reported the greatest impact on feeling empowered to make their own spaces safer for their students.

Conclusions

Surveys conveyed a journey from awareness to empowerment through participation in a *Giving Voice* forum. Many participants reported feeling uncomfortable or afraid to speak up in their own classes, prior to the forum. They reported the forum helped them to not only recognize issues of oppression but also the relevance, regardless of the subject matter of their course. They became conscious of students feeling they had no other choice than to remain silent in wake of comments made in class. With newfound consciousness to not avoid diversity issues or possible difficult dialogues in conjunction with the need to give voice to these students, participants recognized the necessity to create a safe space. Several faculty and graduate assistants talked about making sure everyone felt comfortable, supported, or at least safe to speak their mind in class. This concept was strongly influenced by the *Talkback* Phase during the *Giving Voice* forums.

References

Boal, A. (1992). *Games for actors and non-actors* (A. Jackson, Trans.). Routledge.

Sue, D., Lin, A., Torino, G., Capodilupo, C., & Rivera, D. (2009). Racial microaggressions and difficult dialogues on race in the classroom. *Cultural Diversity and Ethnic Minority Psychology*, *15*(2), 183–190.

Unruh, L. & McCord, D. (2010). Personality traits and beliefs about diversity in preservice teachers. *Individual Differences Research*, *8*(1), 1–7.

12 *Giving Voice* Evolving

Script Focus

"Real change, enduring change, happens one step at a time" (Ginsburg, 1993, p. 122). The concept of *Giving Voice* is applicable to a variety of issues. The troupe has explored issues concerning race, LGBTQ+, gender, religion, politics, socioeconomics, and abilities, to name a few. The scenarios have been explored through a variety of settings, including classrooms, offices, breakrooms, social service centers, company meetings, public safety situations, and churches. Oppression and microaggressions cross many areas of life. The key is the characters who share, on a personal level, how they are affected by something that may seem trivial to others. The calmness of these personal communications in a safe environment allows for true communication, especially listening. Courageous conversations are the effective results that bring about meaningful change.

Boal believed strongly in the ability for theatre to teach and to promote social change. His work and his techniques were very influential in social justice and remain so. Boal used theatre in streets, factories, legislatures, churches, and any place that needed light shed on issues and where people could participate in finding solutions to a variety of problems, such as bullying, drugs, illiteracy, sexual abuse, gender, and racial discrimination. These techniques, in some form or another, are now used worldwide to affect positive change. The key is the audience, who do not sit passively watching, but who are invited to intervene.

While *Giving Voice* has explored a wide variety of situations, there are more to be addressed. Sometimes it is old negatives in a new form. *Giving Voice* is mostly about resisting ignorance. We believe that most people have a good heart, and when or if given a chance to understand, there can be change. Obstacles come from those who think they already know all about the issues and resist change. A major advantage of this type of theatre is the flexibility to be transformed by practitioners based on the needs of the group.

The *Giving Voice* Project's original script, *American History*, was focused mainly on racial issues, along with homophobia and sexism in a university

DOI: 10.4324/9781032676883-12

setting. The intended audience was faculty and staff. This first script focused on racial issues but also included some LGBTQ+ issues. The characters were able to personalize how they were affected by microaggressions from other characters in the scenario. Then during *Talkbacks*, they could not only further elaborate on what the audience witnessed but bring in additional stories of oppression. The characters could also share what they needed to feel safe in the classroom setting of the scenario. While they did not give specifics on what should be said and done during the Interventions, they revealed enough for audience members to contemplate how they might accomplish the goal described.

Although our original focus was on professional development for teachers, we were soon being asked to work with various student groups. Rather than create a whole new script, we decided to adapt the current *American History* script. Since the focus was not only on what teachers say but also on what their students say, it was fairly easy to have the teacher character become a "student leader." This could be a graduate assistant or simply another class member whom the teacher chose to lead the group. The title of the script with students-only characters became *Study Group*.

After holding a forum as a workshop at our university's Collaborative Diversity Conference, we began receiving requests from various organizations, businesses, and other universities. Depending on the group requesting the forum and their goals, we started adopting different approaches to forums but with the basics of our regular forums. Our goals include recognition of oppression, understanding the "other," and allowing audience members to try their ideas for intervention in a safe environment. The following are examples of various forums and their approaches in meeting these goals.

Bureaucracy

Bureaucracy was our first deviation from our traditional forum. Our county juvenile justice organization requested us to address issues that clients had encountered. In order to cover a variety of situations we decided rather than a single script we could develop a series of short vignettes to use for discussion and in some cases intervention practice. These included scenarios such as a Career Counselor who makes assumptions based on a person's gender, age, or ability to get the education needed, a clerk being kind to a young white male but then very unforgiving to a person of color for the same infraction, or a worker speaking loudly and slowly to someone they assumed did not speak English.

Advisement

After the success of using short vignettes with the county juvenile justice organization, we decided to use it for our next specialized request. The Advising Center asked for our help with complaints from students on how advisors were reacting to some recurring situations. These involved advisors recommending a Black student not take an African American Studies course, since they "already have a knowledge base…." After the student explains why they think it would be interesting, the advisor comments that maybe it is a good idea since it "could make for an easier semester."

Another scenario involves a student asking their advisor to move to a different dorm room. The student explains he does not feel comfortable, cannot focus on homework, and is afraid to go to sleep at night. The advisor asks if the roommate has threatened him. He explains his roommate is gay, but he has not done or said anything threatening and believes it is only a matter of time.

In contrast, another scenario involves a student who does not think college is for them. Through questioning, the student shares they like their classes and learning. They just do not feel like they belong. Eventually, it is revealed they are gay, and their roommate is not very pleasant. The roommate has friends over who talk derogatorily, knowing they can be heard. When the advisor suggests getting a new roommate, the student explains he has walked across campus and has had a homophobic slur yelled at them. The incredulous advisor asks, "That's happened here?" The student merely replies, "Multiple times."

Break Room

Our first major change was for an Economic Summit that wanted us to address oppression in business settings, such as sexism, ageism, ableism, in addition to homophobia, and racism. Again, using personal narrative, a script was developed called *Break Room* (see Appendix M). Stories included women being asked to empty the trash cans and clean the break areas. At the same time, only the men were asked to help unload the shipments which sometimes included getting extra pay. A male employee keeps asking a female coworker to go out on a date even after being clearly turned down. A promotion was given to the same male employee over the female he harasses. The female employee had worked at the business longer, and she actually trained the male employee given the promotion. Later it comes out that he socializes with the manager at bars while watching ballgames.

Chalk Talk

During the second year of *Giving Voice*, I found myself inundated with texts from members of the *Giving Voice* Troupe. Some of the texts included pictures of chalk writing on the campus sidewalks. The writing was to advertise a speaker coming to campus later that week. The speaker was a controversial figure who used inflammatory language which included an especially offensive use of religion to attack members of the LGBTQ+ community and a political party. Aside from some "accidentally" spilled water on some of these chalk writings and some submitted complaints to the powers that be, we decided *Giving Voice* needed to take on the taboo subjects of religion and politics through a new script. This resulted in the script titled *Chalk Talk* (see Appendix N).

Widget Company

One of our first major challenges outside of educational settings was for the international company, John Deere Reman. We were asked to develop a forum that would address issues that came to light in an annual survey of workers. I prepared by examining the survey results, especially the comments, which were much more clarifying than the statistical outcomes. Using the information, I developed an outline for a script. The outline guided the troupe as they improvised the workshopping of the script. We then presented the forum at the company's international leadership seminar for top managers from around the world. The feedback from the participants was complimentary. Some discussed how seeing these situations played out and hearing some of the comments and thoughts of their workers were very effective. The majority agreed the forum gave an understanding beyond the survey results.

Shade

At the recommendation of a colleague, *Giving Voice* was asked to be a spotlight feature at the National Art Education Association conference. Much of the research and narrative input was already done through art and by art education majors at the university. They shared a variety of microaggressions they experienced in high school, especially for their art interest. Additionally, I met with various high school art teachers and students to address issues currently found at the high school level. The script addressed microaggressions as being labeled as "weird," LGBTQ+, or not a real career to pursue.

Another layer to the script added racial issues as the group of student characters were to brainstorm ideas for a mural project for Martin Luther King, Jr., Day. This was shortly after the killing of Black teenager, Trayvon Martin. This script was the first to incorporate the name of a Black victim, in this case, by a neighborhood watch volunteer, who had been acquitted. This, in turn, allowed comments about how it was not the first time an innocent young Black man had been killed.

A main *Talking Point* for one of the characters was about why parents of Black children must have "the talk" about how to deal with the police if they encounter them. White characters expressed how foreign this idea was to them. They did not understand the "big deal." One white female character, however, talked about being in the back seat with two friends in the front seat, including the driver who was a young Black man. A police officer pulled them over as they left Taco Bell. The officer asked the white female in the back if she was okay.

Ferguson

Incorporating Trayvon Martin into a script was the first time the troupe used a victim's name. Sadly, it would not be the last time. Unfortunately, we found we could easily update scripts by simply changing or adding new names and locations. On August 9, 2014, an unarmed Black teenager, Michael Brown, was shot and killed by a police officer in Ferguson, Missouri, a suburb of St. Louis. His body remained in the street for four hours.

Just over a week later, classes started at the university and the *Giving Voice* Troupe was back together. While the killing of Michael Brown affected all of us, it hit home for some of the troupe members who were from Ferguson and nearby Florissant. We started by allowing anyone the opportunity to share what they were going through. We listened. After much sharing, discussion, and more listening, we decided we needed to rewrite or create a new script.

While we kept the script title of *American History*, we made major changes in the script and *Talking Points* for audience *Talkback* discussions. These *Talking Points* ranged from how it feels to be the only person of color in a class, to sharing how it felt to be a person of color and being followed in a store. Students of color were able to share how scary it was to be stopped or approached by police even when certain they had done nothing wrong. These *Talking Points* were contrasted with white characters sharing nice elementary memories of police officers coming to their schools. Since the Black Lives Matter movement had become more prominent at this time, we incorporated dialogue explaining why countering with "All lives matter" was not appropriate. This newly revised *American History* script became even more powerful with the *Talking Points* that were shared.

Throwaway Youth

An unusual request came from the author of a new book, *Throwaway Youth* (Fairbank, 2016) about the unhoused teenagers in our area. After in-depth research and interviews of local youths, who were without a home, the author's book had the personal narratives that were shared. This was the key for *Giving Voice* to help the author with the launch of the book. The book did not lend itself to a typical forum. Instead, we developed a reading of parts of the book. Troupe members took on the voices of the characters in the book, based on real young people. Members told the stories of how these young people came to be without homes and what life was like trying to survive on their own.

These voices shared how a parent had passed away and then was replaced by someone who was abusive. "He was abusive physically, mentally, sexually, everything. He would abuse my mother physically and yet she wouldn't believe me when I told her what he did to me." Another teenage character told of striking his mother when he was 12 after she spanked him to the point that he could not take it anymore. "They took me out of school and imprisoned me in my room until we moved out two years later. They'd give me toast with butter and water to eat. I was literally confined to my room and bathroom."

Others described neglect due to parents being on drugs and not having anything in the house to eat. Another recalled being beaten often.

> We got beat. My uncle was a cowboy so he used belts. I don't know if you have ever seen a cowboy belt but it's really thick, and he had the embroidered ones. He would leave them in the sink to soak up water and then beat us with them. He would just find excuses to beat us. We would get beaten for breathing too loud or sitting too close to the TV or whatever.

Many, all genders, shared about sexual abuse being the main reason for running away. Others were kicked out, especially if they were found out to be gay, while others were merely abandoned. Surviving involved stealing shampoo from a local store and then going to an apartment complex to wash. On the other end of the survival spectrum, a young girl explained, "At 14, I was kicked out of the house completely. I was forced to live with older men so that I would be able to survive because at 14 you can't really live on your own." Some joined gangs in order to survive. As one explained, "They didn't have parents, either. We shared that bond – not having real parents. And we also bonded over drugs. We just wanted to escape."

Having troupe members literally be those voices was a powerful experience for the audience. The characters ended by describing how they do not feel seen, much less cared about by the rest of the community. They explained how "homeless youth tend to hide among us. They tend to blend into the background and walk in the shadows." The final statements of the youth included telling they are here, they do exist, and they do matter. Their final directive was to reach out to them. "After all, we're just children."

Training University Security Officers

Several short scenarios were developed to train university security officers based on complaints and troupe member experiences. There was a focus on race, the LGBTQ+ community, and sexual harassment complaints. Members would stage a scenario where security was called, then the officers were allowed to practice how to handle the situation and not escalate it. Some of the scenarios included a same-sex couple arguing loudly, called in by a neighbor.

Another was a student who was being "cat called" and having sexual comments made to her while walking across campus. This had been a problem with some officers not taking it seriously and even indicating this was a compliment. Another situation involved a male student in a science lab setting who sexually harassed a female. The harassment started with comments, continued by asking for dates, even after being turned down, escalated to inappropriate touching, and finally assault with a forced kiss.

Other *Giving Voice* forums have included Health Care professionals, Human Resource workers, the Department of Natural Resources, Behavioral Health professionals, and Ministries, to name a few. Additionally, we have presented at national conferences, such as Public Relations Society of America, Criminology and Criminal Justice Conference, National Conference on Race and Ethnicity, and National Association of Diversity Officers in Higher Education. We developed a special business script for the National Association for Women in Communication called *No Offense*. It seems whenever the words, *no offense*, are used they either precede or follow something offensive.

Giving Voice type forums can be a very effective way to address a variety of issues. Some of these issues may seem insignificant until the person affected is allowed to share what they go through. This is even more powerful for the more obvious or egregious comments. This style of theatre allows for learning and understanding in a calm and safe manner. An important lesson troupe members learn is to listen and not react with aggression, since that only leads to more aggression. Communication is key.

References

Fairbank, N. (2016). *Throwaway youth: Stories of Springfield's homeless teens*. Moon City Press.

Ginsburg, R. (1993, July 20). *Nomination Hearings for Supreme Court Justices*. https://www.govinfo.gov/content/pkg/GPO-CHRG-GINSBURG/pdf/GPO-CHRG-GINSBURG.pdf

Appendix M

Giving Voice **Break Room**

(for the following script, Tiffany and Mary are African Americans)

(TIFFANY enters, looks around looks at her watch shrugs, picks up some papers and starts organizing them to file. Sits in seat 1)

(SHANNON and JOSHUA enter)

JOSHUA:	So what did you end up doing last night, Shannon?
SHANNON:	Uh, nothing exciting, Joshua. We went to that new movie, *Battlefield: LA.*
JOSHUA:	How did you like it?
SHANNON:	It was so gay. It was just a huge sensory overload – just messed up???
TIFFANY:	Good Morning Joshua, Shannon.
JOSHUA:	Hi Tiffany.
SHANNON:	Hi.
TIFFANY:	Do either of you know why we are here, why this meeting is so early? I hope it doesn't take too long. I have a lot of papers to file.
JOSHUA:	I really don't know. Why do you always have to do the filing?

(TIFFANY shrugs)

SHANNON:	*(Sits in seat 2, takes some of the papers from Tiffany and helps organize)* I do it some and so does Rashonda.
TIFFANY:	Hey, I love your shoes.
JOSHUA:	*(Sits in seat 3)*
SHANNON:	Thanks.

(RASHONDA enters with TED)

RASHONDA:	*(kindly by firmly)* Ted, for the last time, I am just not interested in going out with you.
JOSHUA:	Good Morning Rashonda, *(a little less enthusiastically)* Ted.

RASHONDA: *(Sits in seat 4)* Hi Joshua.

(TED makes JOSHUA vacate chair by RASHONDA)

TED: Josh, don't throw off my game. *(JOSHUA just looks at him)* Seriously, you know you're not interested in the lady.

JOSHUA: *(gets up and stands to side of Rashonda, mutters)* Your only game is fantasy football.

(TED sits next to RASHONDA)

RASHONDA: Ted, you're a tool.

TED: Hey, Josh knows I'm just kidding. Don't be so sensitive. Now, where were we…Rashonda, you should be flattered I'm asking you out. Big changes are coming, You need to start being nicer to me. *(pause)* So when are we going out?

RASHONDA: We are not and it is inappropriate for you to keep asking.

TIFFANY: Ted, do you know why are we here?

SHANNON: There is a lot of stuff to be done in the store and we are just wasting time sitting here.

TED: You will find out. *(looks at watch and gets up to leave)* you'll find out as soon as Rick gets here.

(RASHONDA motions for JOSHUA to sit back down beside her)

RASHONDA: You really shouldn't let him push you around like that.

JOSHUA: Whatever. He and Rick do it all the time.

RASHONDA: Then you need to tell Tamara. I'll go with you if you want.

(RICK enters)

RICK: Hi, may I have everyone's attention? Ted *(exchanges fist bumps with TED, then TED exits)*, Tiffany *(to RASHONDA)*, Josh, Shannon, *(then stumbles saying RASHONDA when looks at Tiffany, who is working with papers, again)*

RICK: *(somewhat harsh to Tiffany)* Roshanda?!

TIFFANY: *(looks up)* Tiffany

RASHONDA: I'm Rashonda.

RICK: Oh, yeah, right…. Thank you all for coming in so early, I appreciate it.

First, I want to let you know that Bill is the new store manager.

SHANNON: What?

RICK: Yeah, Bill is now store manager.

SHANNON: What happened to Tamara?

RICK: She's working at Washington Street store now

TIFFANY: Really? She didn't even say anything to us.

(TED enters)

TED: So, Rick did you tell them about prego yet? That she'll be a real worker now!

SHANNON: Wait, What is going on?

RICK: Tamara's not managing the Washington Street store, she's just working there.

TED: So, what do you guys think?

RASHONDA: We are not all "guys" and I think Tamara shouldn't be working on Washington St. She's going to give birth. It's the worst neighborhood and it's so far from her house…

SHANNON: It's like she was demoted.

TIFFANY: She's worked at this store a long time. She even hired me.

TED: I'm not talking about her, I'm talking about Rick, he's our new assistant manager now, isn't that awesome!

JOSHUA: *(apprehensive)* Great.

SHANNON: I started working here before you did.

RASHONDA: And Tiffany was working here before Shannon. Tiffany is responsible, she is always here. She helps everyone. Didn't she show you the ropes?

RICK: Okay, but I have been working closely with Bill. He was already showing me the ropes as Asst. Manager, so they thought it would be easier just to hire me.

RASHONDA: No offense, but this just doesn't make sense. Why wasn't anyone told about this. The application process or anything…

RICK: I already know how to do this stuff.

SHANNON: But I also already know *how to do all this stuff.*

RICK: You don't know about stocking and, anyway, Bill recommended me.

TIFFANY: Shouldn't we have had a chance to apply for management or something?

RICK: Hey, I have a family to support.

(BILL enters room)

BILL: Good morning! Really glad to see everyone, bright and early this morning. I'm sure you heard the good news. I want you to know that Rick has my full support, and is ready to hit the ground running. Congratulations Rick…

SHANNON: Why was Rick made Assistant Manager?

BILL: *(ignoring question)* Let's all come together and make this the best store. Alright, huddle up like the team we are. It's going to be great.

RICK: Go Team on three, ONE….TWO….THREE……

EVERYONE: Go Team!

BILL: Great. I have to go to a meeting to get to. Have a good day. *(Fist bumps for Rick and Ted)*

RICK: *(following Bill)* Hey, man, I thought you would be around more, especially my first day and all.

BILL: You'll be fine. Remember, you are in charge and to delegate. You can call me but… I hired you to handle things. *(exits)*

RICK: Ted, I need you to watch the front while we continue this meeting,

TED: Okay, I got it.

RICK: Thanks.

SHANNON: So what about your old position? Are we going to have to take on more hours?

RICK: I have been given the authority to hire a new employee. The sign's up out front and I would like to give you a say in who we hire, so does anyone know of anyone? *(to RASHONDA)* Tiffany?

JOSHUA: Oh, I know somebody who is looking for a job and they would be a good worker.

RICK: Okay Josh, give me some background.

JOSHUA: He picks up on things fast, reliable, he's a hard working…

RICK: Oh *(on hearing "he" interrupts)*-okay, okay; tell him to fill out an application.

TED: Hey Rick. We have someone out front and, uh, they want to do a return. They're really kinda angry right now. Do you know the code…

RICK: Ted, just take care of it. I'm kinda busy right now.

TED: They're just really mad and I don't know the code to…

RICK: Look, just go up there and take care of it!

TIFFANY: *(whispers)* 1356

TED: *(quietly)* Thank you.

SHANNON: Oh, My aunt just moved into town and she is looking for a job.

RICK: She's your aunt-how old is she? I mean, tell me a little bit about her, Is she from your mom or dad's side of the family?

TIFFANY: What?

RICK: Is she black or white?

JOSHUA: Does that matter?

RASHONDA: I don't think you are suppose to ask that?

RICK: I get asked that all the time. Its' just natural curiosity, because you don't see very many mixed races here.

RASHONDA: You don't see many Arabs either.

SHANNON: And what makes you think I'm some sort of "Oreo" anyway?

TIFFANY: It doesn't matter.

(TED walks in with MARY)

TED:	The sign's paying off already. We have an applicant… *(stays back to "watch" store)*
MARY:	Mary. Actually, I saw the posting online last night, downloaded and filled out an application (*hands Rick an application)*. I am hoping since I worked at similar store…
RICK:	*(Giving MARY the brush off)* Okay, thank you.
MARY:	*(shaking RICK's hand)* Also, I am a marketing major and I have a lot of experience…
RICK:	Okay, okay, we'll call you.
MARY:	Oh, okay, thank you so much *(MARY leaves the room)*
TED:	Hey, there's a code 10, want to check it out?
RICK:	Not now, Ted. What are you thinking, man? I know you just graduated high school but… go back to the front.
TED:	*(sort of whispering)* Alright, no big deal *(glances at Rashonda, dejected, exits)*
TIFFANY:	Oh yeah, I've been meaning to ask someone, what is a Code 10?
RICK:	Don't worry about it, it's no big deal. We're doing away with it.
SHANNON:	As the new Assistant Manager, you should/know…
JOSHUA:	It means "Hot Chick"/
TIFFANY:	*(quiet, indignant disbelief)/*Wow
SHANNON:	/Great, this is 2011/and we still…
RASHONDA:	/Oh, of course that's what that means. Do you know how inappropriate that is?
RICK:	Thanks Josh. What do you care? You know what, it's not a big deal so let's just move on, okay? *(to RASHONDA)* Tiff… *(stops, realizes wrong name)*
RASHONDA:	Rashonda.
RICK:	Do you have an applicant?
RASHONDA:	*(shakes her head "no")*
TIFFANY:	I do. Actually, have a couple of people in mind that would be very good.
RICK:	*(not really interested)* Have them fill out an application.

(TED enters with KAYLA)

TED:	You have another applicant.
KAYLA:	Hi, my name is Kayla.
RICK:	Hi, nice to meet you.
KAYLA:	Nice to meet you.
RICK:	Do you have an application?
KAYLA:	No, I just saw the sign and…
RICK:	Well, let's save some time and just have an interview since you're here. I'll be right back.

(RICK and KAYLA exit. RASHONDA, SHANNON, JOSHUA, and TIFFANY look at each other)

TIFFANY: Ted, tell us what's going on. Why did Tamara move?

TED: *(sits in Rick's chair)* Listen guys. Let's be real, Tamara is huge now.

TIFFANY: She's pregnant.

TED: I know, she looks like she's off that show *16 and Pregnant.*

JOSHUA: She's 27 and married.

TED: Hey, this is better for her. Besides girls are better at jobs like answering phones, cleaning, and filing.

RASHONDA: Oh, I'll make sure that is all I do from now on.

TED: *(stands and moves by Rashonda)* Just kidding. Don't get all feminist on me. Oh, that's why you won't go out with me. You're a lesbian. I should have known, short hair…*(laughs)*

(KAYLA enters)

SHANNON: Are you looking for Rick or something?

KAYLA: No, I actually just got hired. So, Rick said to come back in here and meet your guys.

JOSHUA: Congratulations, I'm Josh.

KAYLA: Hi, I'm Kayla. *(they shake hands)*

RASHONDA: Rashonda (*shakes hands)*

SHANNON: Shannon. *(an awkward half shake/slide fingers/fist bump)*

TIFFANY: Tiffany. *(awkward fist bump of some sort)*

(KAYLA moves to Ted who is standing near Rashonda as RICK enters)

RICK: Sorry, I had to fill out some paperwork. I'm sure you all met Kayla, our new employee. (*puts out his hand, which KAYLA awkwardly takes)* Kayla, give a little spin, show everyone what the new store look looks like.

KAYLA: (*quietly)* Okay (*as she turns around still holding Rick's hand)*

RASHONDA: Does she have more than just the store look?

KAYLA: Oh yeah, I have a lot of experience, I've worked in a tanning salon. Actually I shopped here, actually… *(doesn't get to tell them about spying for a rival store where she worked before)*

SHANNON: Oh, she shopped here. Good job, Rick.

JOSHUA: How old are you?

KAYLA: Almost 18.

RICK: (*nonchalantly)* When's your birthday?

TED: So, let's all get started. You guys can start straightening up out front. Me and Rick will go do the stocking.

TIFFANY: (*to Rick)* About that, Rick. You, Ted, and, before, Bill always do the stocking. Doesn't stocking pay extra, especially if you are doing it off hours?

RICK:	*(snaps at TIFFANY)* Because it needs to get done. Tiffany, right? Any other useless questions?
SHANNON:	I'd like the extra money.
JOSHUA:	I'd like to just to get it organized. Right now, you can't find anything.
KAYLA:	I would be interested in earning extra money.
TED:	There's a lot of heavy lifting back there. It's a guy thing to do.
RASHONDA:	That's retarded
TIFFANY:	You never ask Joshua to do it.
TED:	(*aside to Rick but loud enough to be heard by the others)* I said it was a "guy" thing, not a "gay" thing. (*laughs)* Well, maybe Rashonda could help us out back there.
RASHONDA:	(*stands)* Rick, say something./Do something about this…
/JOSHUA:	(*stands)* Just leave Rashonda alone…
/SHANNON:	(*stands)* Any of us could stock…
RICK:	SIT DOWN … SIT DOWN..

(All sit as…)

TIFFANY:	(*stands)* All I meant was…
RICK:	Tiffany. Stop being disruptive. Look, you two *(indicating TIFFANY and SHANNON)* have been here the longest, right? You go show her the ropes.

(TIFFANY begins to rise. No one else moves)

RICK:	If you value your jobs…

(TIFFANY, SHANNON, RASHONDA start exiting. JOSHUA indicates for KAYLA to follow)

(RICK motions for TED to exit, then sits down)

Performed by the Giving Voice Troupe, Spring of 2012 with the following actors in the roles:

BILL	***Drew Irwin***
MARY	***Kanome Jones***
JOSHUA	***Rolo Rodriguez***
RASHONDA	***Samantha Long***
SHANNON	***Dannie Patrick***
RICK	***Ariel Forste***
TIFFANY	***Leah Ricketts***
TED	***Corey Hollander***
KAYLA	***Sarah Hohne***

Appendix N

Giving Voice ________________________________ ***Chalk Talk***

(DANIEL is standing near seat #1 going over notes. AUDREY and MORGAN enter room talking.)

AUDREY: Morgan, one of them compared liberals to Islamic terrorists!
MORGAN: Seriously?
AUDREY: and one of them said, (*reading from picture of the chalk writing on phone*) "Even Islamic Terrorists don't hate America like liberals do" *(sits in seat #2)*
DANIEL: So, someone else saw the sidewalk chalkings.
MORGAN: *(Overlapping DANIEL, as she sits in seat #3)* Oh my gosh, Audrey…what did you do?

(CHELLY enters)

CHELLY: *(with enthusiasm, although not sincere)* Yay, we have a meeting today! *(sits in seat #7)* Hey Audrey. Hey Daniel. *(leaves out MORGAN)* What's up?

(AUDREY, DANIEL, and MORGAN greet CHELLY.)

DANIEL: I am going to check to see who gave approval for that.

(Zak and Kristen enter)

KRISTEN: *(to Morgan as she sits in seat #4)* What's going on?
MORGAN: Oh, hi Kristen. Audrey's upset about those chalkings all over the sidewalks.
ZAK: *(sits in seat #5)* Why? What's the big deal?/Freedom of speech and all.
AUDREY: They shouldn't be allowed, Zak./That's the big deal.
CHELLY: (*Overlapping from "Zak"*)/Yeah, I saw one comparing gay marriage to civil rights for black people or something. What's up with that?

AUDREY: Yeah, see, Chelly and Kristen know what I'm talking about.

KRISTEN: (*a quick look/reaction to AUDREY's comment then continues*) There is freedom of speech.

MORGAN: (*Overlapping from "about")*/Wait. Is that the one that got you so upset?/*(AUDREY gives MORGAN a look)*

CHELLY: (*Overlapping from "talking"*)/No, I just meant I saw it… I don't understand…

(ALEX enters)

ZAK: Hey Alex, it's about time you got here. We need some more testosterone here to break up this CATFIGHT. *("catfight noises")*

ALEX: Catfight?! Ladies, please! Everyone can calm down. Ladies, I'm here. It's going to be okay.

(makes elaborate gesture for the ladies who just look at him, roll eyes, etc. He then sits in seat #6)

KRISTEN: *(to ZAK and ALEX).* You two should go do special Olympics together.

DANIEL: (*standing behind seat #4)* Okay, let's get started. We need to decide a group to do community service with. Ideas?

ALEX: By the way, does anyone want to go with me to hear a speaker tonight?

ZAK: Who's the speaker?

ALEX: I don't know. I just know I get extra credit in one of my classes *(change to "it will look good if I go" depending on audience)* and I don't want to go by myself.

ZAK: Why? Are you a pussy?

ALEX: (*laughing)* Shut up, faggot.

(*Females have varying subtle reactions, especially between each other)*

MORGAN: Hey, so wait. Did you say you are going to hear the speaker tonight?

ALEX: Yeah.

KRISTEN: Isn't that who the sidewalk chalk is advertising?

DANIEL: Oh yeah, that far right conservative…

MORGAN: Wait. Republican?

AUDREY: What?!/Why would you support that?

ALEX: Cause I need the extra credit. I got jewed out of my last test grade, so…

CHELLY: Hey Alex, um, I'll go with you to the speaker if you'll come to New Leaf with me tonight.

ALEX: What's New Leaf?

CHELLY: A Christian youth group we started. We do, like, singing and some prayer, worship and stuff like that. You guys can all come if you want.

KRISTEN: (*supporting CHELLY)* It will be fun.

DANIEL: (*trying to get back on track)* That's great. Now who can throw out a name of an organization we can work with?

KRISTEN: The young Republicans are picking up trash this weekend. We can join them.

DANIEL: Okay…uh…anybody else have any other group?

AUDREY: Of course Republicans support that speaker. Now it makes sense./Republicans and hate together as usual…

ZAK: /Big surprise and they are the Christians. I'm surprised you're *(to KRISTEN)* into that.

KRISTEN: (*supporting CHELLY)* I enjoy New Leaf when I have the time. You all should come.

ZAK: No, I'm talking about Republicans not Baptists. That doesn't surprise me.

AUDREY: Organized religion drives me crazy.

DANIEL: Which is why we need to not talk about that and find a group for community service.

MORGAN: Guys, I think we should just accept everybody for whatever they are, okay? Actually, I'm in a group that doesn't like organized religion. We're still Christian but everyone is more than welcome to come to our group also.

CHELLY: *(mumbles)* … not a real Christian….

AUDREY: *(to MORGAN)* Did you not see the sidewalk chalk about them saying all Democrats and liberals are atheist?

ZAK: That's right. Democrats are un-American, bleeding heart atheists who think government is the answer to everything and Republicans are Christian patriots who don't believe in big government interference…or science/…or birth certificates. *(laughs)*

AUDREY: (*Overlap at "interference"*) Except when it comes to a woman's body or who gets married.

CHELLY: (*Overlapping at* "science") What?!/

DANIEL: (*Overlapping from "What?!"*)/That's not true.

(MORGAN: (*Overlapping from "woman's body"*) What is wrong with wanting to protect an unborn child?

(Several chime in)

ALEX: Chill. Chill. What Morgan is trying to say is Republicans don't have a monopoly on Christianity. Some Democrats are Christian.

MORGAN: That's true Alex, but …

ALEX: She just means Republicans are associated with Christianity.

AUDREY: And anyone else is going to hell?

CHELLY: (*looking at Morgan)* Only if they are not a born again Christian.

DANIEL: Let's move on. I talked to my Dad and he said that we could work with FOCUS. They said we could help with their project coming up.

KRISTEN: What's FOCUS?

DANIEL: You know, the LGBT organization.

ZAK: *(aside: laughs to ALEX)* What a choice, Republicans or *(makes limp wrist gesture).*

ALEX: *(aside: laughing)* You know there won't be both.

CHELLY: Let's work with FOCUS.

KRISTEN: I am fine with either one. Let's just decide.

ALEX: *(to CHELLY)* Wait. You will work with gays? Don't you think they are going to hell?

CHELLY: Yeah, technically but that doesn't mean I can't hang out with them. At least they won't be hitting on me. *(looks at ALEX)* So, that's a plus.

DANIEL: What about the girls?

AUDREY: I vote to help the group that's picking up trash. Then we can start with the garbage written on the sidewalks. Let's clean that off first.

ZAK: Why does it bother you so much?

KRISTEN: That's free speech.

ALEX: Kristen's right. Ever hear of the first amendment?

MORGAN: But Audrey has a point about the messages on the sidewalk. They're extremely in your face.

KRISTEN: It's still freedom of speech.

AUDREY: No. It's hate speech.

ALEX: *(to KRISTEN)* It compares gay marriage to the civil rights movement. I am surprised you are defending it.

KRISTEN: What?

MORGAN: Audrey's the one that's really upset about that. *(everyone looks puzzled)*

ALEX: *(to AUDREY)* Why is she upset? She's not bl… *(starts to say "black" but realizes awkward)*

KRISTEN: Excuse me?

DANIEL: Let's move on. The groups so far are the Young Republicans and FOCUS. Since we are not finding any agreement, there is one other group I talked to…just a few blocks down…the Mosque?

ZAK: I think you mean the Sikh Temple?

CHELLY: Muslims? No.

KRISTEN:	Sikhs are not Muslim. Isn't it called a gurdwara? *(pronounced* gɜː(r)dwɑːrə *"good – wur – a")*
CHELLY:	Oh, okay.
DANIEL:	Yes, they welcome anyone.
ALEX:	At least the ugly women are covered up.
ZAK:	How about my professor's church group? Dr. Bates gives extra credit for coming to his church, so he would probably give credit if I brought help for a community service project.
MORGAN:	Wait, isn't he the one that puts down women?
KRISTEN:	Yeah, you told us he said something about women only move up by lying on their backs?

(ALEX and ZAK laugh)

AUDREY:	Wait. Why can't we help with the Islamic group??
CHELLY:	I know don't want to work with a group that hates every other religious belief....
ZAK:	Might as well go with Democrats. (*laughs*)
MORGAN:	Democrats are not anti-religion and Republicans...
AUDREY:	Your right. Republicans are tearing this country apart with their hate./It's un-American...
CHELLY:	No, un-American are Muslims who...
KRISTEN:	There are plenty of Muslim Americans. I'm not helping a professor who runs down women...
ZAK:	Alex, got a dollar? We can make it rain.
DANIEL:	No one's going to make it rain. So, FOCUS?
ALEX:	Well, you girls work with the Glee Club and we'll build houses with Habitat for Humanity like real men, am I right?
DANIEL:	Actually, there is a group working for Habitat for Humanity is FOCUS.

Developed by the *Giving Voice* Troupe, Spring of 2012 with the following actors in the roles:

DANIEL	***Rolo Rodriguez***
MORGAN	***Tessa Harbaugh***
AUDREY	***Sarah Hohne***
CHELLY	***Dannie Patrick***
KRISTEN	***Aryiel Everett***
ZAK	***Chris Porcelli***
ALEX	***Corey Hollander***

13 Troupe Members

Troupe Ensemble

Never underestimate the power of a small group of committed people to change the world.

In fact, it is the only thing that ever has (Mead, n.d.). Dedicated troupe members are the key to positive change. They must also be prepared to change themselves. However, the effect of being in the troupe should not be underestimated. Troupe members, themselves, must be prepared to change. This was something I had not realized when I started *Giving Voice*. As we started to hold forums, followed by a debriefing, I started to recognize the changes expressed by the troupe members. This was also prevalent during discussions of the exercises they did while developing an ensemble. The change in the students who continued in the troupe for two, three, or four years was very open about the effect of the exercises and how their reactions had changed over the years when engaging in the same exercises a year later with new members. This is made possible mainly by the trust that is developed within the troupe. Establishing and nurturing a safe environment is essential for the troupe members, their work, and their growth.

Conventional semester evaluations were used where some reactions became evident in relation to the structure of *Giving Voice*. A few quotes from troupe member responses follow and are worth noting for those who want to lead a group:

> We were made to feel safe, loved, & comfortable.
>
> I appreciated the challenges, sometimes intense, while keeping us safe emotionally and physically.
>
> We were pushed to our full extent of work, but it felt good.
>
> I love how passionate our leader is and willing to learn with her students.
>
> One of the best things about *Giving Voice* is creating a sense of ensemble. This helps us during forums to know we have each other's back.

DOI: 10.4324/9781032676883-13

> Our leader is great at making us think about who we are and the people around us, but she always makes sure we are ok in the process.
>
> I felt very included and accepted. I cannot say the same for my other classes.
>
> It's a family environment.
>
> It truly is a safe environment. Nowhere else do we get to talk in depth about such important topics.

These responses to standard class evaluations were helpful, but most discoveries about the changes in troupe members came from discussions within the troupe. For this book, I wanted to hear from troupe members and give them voice to what being in the troupe meant to them. The following reflections are in their own words.

Erika

> My time as a *Giving Voice* Warrior is an absolute vital part of my life journey. It had a big influence on how I shaped my world view and fundamental beliefs as a young adult. I grew up as one of few people of color in a conservative area. *Giving Voice* challenged me to confront toxic, ignorant, and biased ideologies I held as well as affirmed that my ethnicity and gender were something to be celebrated, not looked down upon. I learned things I never knew about other people's beliefs and experiences because we as members were challenged to listen to learn, rather than listen to argue or confront. When faced with opposition, we could practice how to de-escalate, disarm, and encourage open dialogue. Above all, I was given the key to true empathy. I learned that true empathy is not a feeling, it is a skill that must be cultivated and maintained. I learned how to embrace people who were different from me and see the world through their eyes. I find that stepping into another person's shoes is a lot easier for me now, even when considering someone's perspective that I don't identify with. *Giving Voice* taught me how to listen, empathize, and turn that into compassion by adding advocacy and action. It is something I will take with me always.

Anna S

> I was a part of Missouri State University's Giving Voice from 2019-2022. It remains one of the most impactful organizations I have ever been a part of and has truly shaped me into the person I am today.

During my freshman year of college, I stumbled upon Giving Voice. All I knew was that it was a theatre organization that created skits addressing different social issues. I was somewhat naive and did not fully grasp the extent of what Giving Voice was and the powerful impact of Augusto Boal's work.

Shortly after Thanksgiving, my childhood best friend's parents had been deported due to lack of documentation. The news broke my heart. It felt like I had lost two of my own family members. I was angry and frustrated with the world for allowing such a thing to happen to a family that had been nothing but supportive, kind, and loving to me throughout my childhood. I didn't know what to do. But then I was introduced to the power of Giving Voice.

Dr. Carol Maples, along with the other troupe members, encouraged me to speak out about the injustice and to delve deeper into the immigration system, listening to stories from people with similar experiences to my friend and her family. Through my research, I gained a new perspective on what it is like to be an undocumented immigrant living in America.

In the early weeks of my involvement with Giving Voice, I came across a powerful quote: "silence is the indicator of approval." Reflecting on my friend and her family's experiences, I faced a crucial choice: to remain silent or to speak out. I chose to use my voice. With the guidance of Dr. Carol Maples and the support of the Giving Voice troupe, we crafted a script addressing the discrimination endured by undocumented immigrants. Our troupe performed this script in front of college and high school audiences across Missouri. Through this endeavor, I had the opportunity to engage in conversations that encouraged people to consider perspectives beyond their own ideologies on immigration.

After each performance, audience members approached me and my troupe with questions. This reinforced my belief that what we were doing was reshaping ideas and helping individuals become more compassionate and empathetic beings.

Giving Voice has made me realize the privilege and responsibility that comes with using my voice. It has helped me understand the significance of standing up against injustice. This understanding has permeated into my daily life and how I educate my own students. I consistently emphasize to them that even the smallest voices can have the greatest impact. I always encourage them to speak up and understand that their voices and their presence truly matter. It has inspired me to create my own Giving Voice organization at my own school.

Kailey

Through *Giving Voice*, I have found and begun to express a great courage, passion, and empathy for myself and the world around me that has afforded me great success in my personal, social, and professional life. I have found that I am now more curious as to the whys behind people's actions and words, and better able to see the world in color rather than black and white, or good and bad. I have learned that people cannot be restricted to either good or evil by means of the characters that we have created together. I have learned that anything and everything can become a means of expressing what needs to be expressed by means of the games that we play. I have learned of the enormous potential that humans have by means of observing my fellow actors and myself grow as a result of the work we do. I have become more well-rounded, more understanding, and kinder to myself and others because of *Giving Voice*. As someone who does not intend to go into theatre professionally, I can confidently say that I think every profession, and every person for that matter, can find something within Theatre for Social Change and Boal style exercises that benefits them both personally and professionally.

Anna M

Giving Voice instilled a sense of belonging in me that I was missing when I joined my sophomore year. The work we do as a troupe has made me a more empathetic and open-minded person and a stronger advocate for issues I am passionate about.

Aryiel

While at my time being a student at Missouri State I had the honor to be a member of the Giving Voice Acting Troupe led by Dr. Carol J. Maples. The Giving Voice acting troupe was an experience that gave me a place I could call home within the theatre program at MoState. Everyone desires a found family and for years they not only provided me with a safe space but a place that I could exist and be deeply human. The challenges we faced… we did them together and with care and respect. This program has guided my steps to truly be who I am today. My advice to anyone who wanted to do this work is to ask question and learn from yours and other lived experiences. This work is essential to shape the lives of not only employees within the corporate world, our amazing folks that are educators, but also the students. CJ's program has guided me to finally pursue my own dream into doing a form of this work within the Kansas City Metro for students in the Kansas City Public School system and Charter Management Organizations. Take the time to dive into this work if you ever get an opportunity and remember to just say "yes, I am open to the change." You will be moved and shaped in ways you never knew theatre could do. Heal, learn, and love. Thank you CJ!

Corey

Beefcake, total bro, jock – all names that were normal in the first few weeks at school. Now I know what most or at least some people would say to this story, oh poor you! and to be honest, they aren't wrong. There's a lot more overt, obvious, and problematic discrimination others faced than me and I knew that at the time but the *Giving Voice* troupe and particularly you looked right at me and said tell me your story and you LISTENED. The other people that eventually joined us listened and heard me out too. I felt vindicated and don't worry, my classmates learned to accept me for who I was and saw a lot more past my initial appearance.

Here I was in the troupe, a young guy among WAY older students than I am. I still follow most of them on social media these days. I learned a lot from how they thought about things from their diverse upbringings. Thinking about this now and being a 'dad' for a little over a year. A lot of those lessons had a profound impact on me and how I will raise my sons. Trying to remember more about our workshops and oh boy did I enjoy those. I had never and still to this day have NEVER seen or participated in ANYTHING like that. Boal/Theatre for the Oppressed/Interactive Performances are the most dynamic I have ever been as an actor. I think there's few if any things that an artist can participate in that are as impactful and transformative as what we did.

That was just the beginning. I remember *really* pushing it. Rehearsals were tough and it wouldn't have been possible without a leader and our guide. We had to know it was safe to go there.

I reflected on myself through the work and more importantly, I listened to others. I listened to my classmates talk about the police growing up, how one was taught they were the helpers and another taught they were the enforcers. The perspectives were real and authentic and they landed with me. We brought these to so many people on our campus. The work was powerful but always safe and I didn't realize to what extent until I matured and entered the workforce. Like many past students I'm not an Actor (shocking!) but I will always look back fondly at the training I received and know I'll find myself back performing someday. I just hope when I do the work I can participate in is half as meaningful as what we did.

The troupe brought its attendees to look someone face to face, in a safe setting, and allow them to see the impact of their words on another. I think everyone would agree that the world has changed in the last 3ish years, pandemic aside, but I don't think anyone would agree exactly how. I feel there'd be a large consensus that would at least agree to me that kindness, empathy and caring about the impact we make on other people seems to be scarce and that's what the troupe cultivated.

Aerrionna

Being in the troupe taught me to love being my black self. Attending predominantly white institutions my whole life was a struggle. A battle. From the way I talked to the music I liked. But, this troupe really helped me realize that being black within itself is luxury and power.

David

Giving Voice meant so much to me. It gave me the ability to see the world from new perspectives. I got to see and learn first-hand of microaggressions in the world and different ways how to fix them. I looked forward to coming to class every day and creating new scripts, having discussions of what is going on in the world and how it affects not only the people in the world but also your fellow classmates. From this I got to learn how to handle situations of microaggressions and also gave the opportunity to all the people we got to perform for. Even if 5 people out of an audience of 20 learned from us that is still 5 people who are going to go out in the world and change it.

Along with everything I just said I also got to make several lifelong friends that I am still in communication with today!

Krissa

In my industry, school, and even peer group, I seldom feel like I have a voice. I have so much to say, and I say it often, but for some reason I don't feel heard. This is a problem for so many of us, no matter how you personally have (or haven't) been marginalized or oppressed/overlooked. Most places don't exist to feel like a safe space, or an environment where people can feel like they have agency or value. Many exist to do the opposite. Only upon being a part of a group that knows the value of giving voices to the voiceless—because it's what each member wants for themselves and wants to give to others—did I understand how invaluable a safe space to create art and share personal experiences was. *Giving Voice*, and everything it has done, has benefited countless people who both aspired to unlearn harmful behaviors and who longed for a conversation that spoke to and of them. But it helps the artists just as much as it helps the "spect-actors," as I've learned. As a neurodiverse individual, a queer individual, a Latina, and just as a person, my burning desire to make a difference in the way the world views and treats people who are different has always been smothered by the incredibly disheartening fact that because of who I am I have never been listened to. *Giving Voice* did its namesake well, because I finally get to be in a space where what I am doesn't matter; where the only thing that people cared about were my words and my intentions. Our stories and our experiences suddenly had value, and we've gotten to teach countless people that their experiences get to have value too. At the end of the day, we get to use our art to make people feel more human, and to unlearn all the things that keep us from seeing each other as just as human. That's the best kind of change that anyone can hope to enact. And think about it; what greater tool has there ever been to appeal to each other's vulnerabilities, empathy, and humanity than the arts. It's our greatest tool to connect with each other. It's how I'm able to be heard. It's how we're all able to be heard. When push comes to shove, our job is to speak to you. And when our job has finished, with any luck, you will have done the most important job of all: you will have listened.

Trish

Giving Voice was one of the biggest and most rewarding challenges as an actor and a person. When playing the oppressor, it is key to fully commit, even if it makes you uncomfortable. Sitting with and learning from my own discomfort pushed me to be a better actor as well as a better human. So thankful for all of the work we did, and I know that it still has shaped the way that I approach the world. Thank you! *Giving Voice* changed my life and made me a better person.

Sarah

Giving Voice has been a place for me to uplift the voices of marginalized communities and hopefully better stigmas against individuals who have not been given platforms to do so themselves. Somewhat selfishly, it has also been a safe and open place for me to finally be myself. For a better part of my life, I grew up going to schools where the majority of students were white, and my teachers were never biracial like me. More importantly, in my classes we never talked about the heritage or experiences of others who weren't part of the majority. I felt my identity slowly slip away and I didn't see myself as a person of color anymore. The Caucasian part of my heritage shone through and unless asked about my middle name or ethnic appearance, I hid a better part of myself from my classmates and teachers.

At the start of college, I told my Giving Voice Class that I was white passing and that a majority of my experiences wouldn't be useful to the class. I was met with kindness and genuine consideration about why I had felt like this. The group not only reaffirmed my life as a biracial individual but they also allowed me a space where I could speak my truth on the matter. Almost 4 years in the group, I have not regretted my decision to join the troupe. I am constantly in awe of the work of the team and their continued dedication to bettering themselves and others. I'm proud and grateful that I get to be in this amazing organization.

Fiona

Giving Voice granted me the opportunity to extend grace to myself and others. I spent so much of my life feeling like I needed to be on the defensive, that when I learned about work where you offer everyone a chance to be heard, seen, and valued, so much opened up in my life. This work challenges you to embrace fierce empathy and compassionate equity. Seeing those doors open up for others – whether in the troupe or a participant in a forum – throughout my time was so rewarding. Giving Voice made me a better listener and leader. I feel equipped to acknowledge bias/harm in my workplace(s) and relationships because of my experience in the troupe. I'm more aware of my own privilege and believe I'm more likely to take advantage of opportunities to help my community because of my time in Giving Voice.

From the Director

As the director of *Giving Voice*, I have the unique opportunity to observe the growth of many of the members through their time in the troupe. Troupe members join to make a positive difference in their world and beyond. Most do not realize how in depth the preparation is to become effective at making that difference. I also get to know their own stories, especially as they become comfortable and trust the other troupe members and me. I get to see the discoveries they make about themselves and audiences. Often, the discoveries include finding their own voice and the ability to call people in with real understanding rather than call them out with anger. During our end-of-season celebrations, we honor the troupe members who are graduating. This is done by giving them a small rose quartz heart. It is a symbol of our goal to touch the hearts of those we encounter. Even more inspiring are the stories that are shared about specific forums, including people that are changed, or time with the troupe, such as extended trips.

Being a part of *Giving Voice* has allowed members to travel all over our nation to present forums. For some, being in the troupe allowed them to fly for the first time. For others, it was their first time even traveling out of the state. *Giving Voice* was invited as a designated Spotlight Presentation for the National Art Education Association Conference in San Diego, CA. This honor gave troupe members an opportunity to present forums and see the sights, including the beautiful Coronado Bay area and historic Hotel del Coronado. What I most loved was presenting forums at conferences in Washington, D.C., giving most of the troupe members their first time experiencing our nation's capital. Being accepted to present at the National Conference on Race and Ethnicity gave us our first trip to Washington, D.C., where we used the *Ferguson* script. Our next honor, taking us to Washington, D.C., was a forum at the National Association of Diversity Officers in Higher Education conference. As with other conferences, this led to being asked to come to other universities across the nation to hold forums. As of this writing, many of the past troupe members have used what they learned being in *Giving Voice* beyond their personal lives. They have used what they learned in their workplace and schools, and some have even started their own versions of *Giving Voice*.

Inspiration, learning, and growth were not limited to *Giving Voice* troupe members. As the director, I constantly learn from and am inspired by troupe members. Their passion to make a positive difference is always impressive and heartening. Society is always changing and the only way to come close to keeping up is by listening. This is especially true for the director to listen as much or more than just talking to young troupe members. I have been fortunate to have worked with some of the finest youth, who give me hope for the future.

Reference

Mead, M. (n.d.). *Smithsonian National Museum of American History*. Retrieved December 18, 2023, from americanhistory.si.edu. Web site: https://americanhistory.si.edu/collections/nmah_1285394

14 Conclusions

Challenges of *Giving Voice* Work

"Darkness cannot drive out darkness: only light can do that. Hate cannot drive out hate: only love can do that" (King, 1964, p. 45). The reward of making a positive difference through work like *Giving Voice* does not come without challenges. Not all audience members are ready to face their own engagement in oppression. While some audience members have a sincere desire to know and understand the wonderfully diverse people who are different from them, others believe they are not the problem. Some are ready to defend themselves rather than acknowledge their own biases or racism. The term racist does not come easily for someone to admit, on any level. Many like to say they do not see color, which means they do not see the person. Others claim they are an ally without fully understanding the meaning.

There have been times, after a forum that the troupe members were very pleased with an audience. They would talk about how well *Talkbacks* went and how good the interventions were from eager volunteers. Then, there have been other times, when the troupe's initial reaction was to be incredulous that the audience was not as engaged or did not have the best of interventions. These times included comments about not being able to believe how bad the audience was or how they just "didn't get it." These were the times to remember those audience members are why we do this work. If everyone caught all the microaggressions and had a positive intervention that improved the situation, then *Giving Voice* would not be necessary. During those times, debriefing becomes even more critical. It is important for the discussion to include specific incidents or comments that the troupe members found frustrating or troublesome. Then, we can look at how we might have responded differently. Sometimes, troupe members need to be reminded of our goal to "call people in" rather than "call people out." That is the difference between communication or shutting down.

Unfortunately, there is a continuing need to educate, address, and confront oppression, including microaggressions. This is not because there is constantly new oppression but because we have not learned from the past. Many

DOI: 10.4324/9781032676883-14

of the scripts developed by *Giving Voice* were adjusted by the setting to fit the audience. The oppressions addressed in the scenarios have been either fairly consistent with only slight differences or include exactly what was part of the first scenario created over 10 years ago. Then there are the parts of a script where only the names of victims have changed or been added to others. At this time, the political climate can be a major challenge to this work. Silence indicates approval. It is a time that voices matter more than ever.

Our scripts over the years attest to the same oppressions that have become a part of our culture, occurring in one form or another, year after year. The political climate has now become another factor, using race, sexual orientation, and gender as cultural divides. The challenges can seem overwhelming at times and society may never grow beyond seeing people as their stereotypes. Stereotypes allow people to dehumanize others. This in turn makes it easier to oppress the "other." Our country is the most polarized I have experienced, with people only listening to like-minded people and like-minded information sources. However, there have been similar times in our past, which ironically, is part of our history that some want to censor. There seems to be a wave of imposed silence on what should be known, from banned books to banned people. While many justify this as protection, others find it an excuse for violence. Words do matter. This polarization has resulted in too many people living in fear and silence. Boal found himself in dangerous times and developed a type of theatre to help navigate what was happening. Through this type of theatre, we can have the conversations so desperately needed among those that are different from each other.

Ironically, weaponizing words has become a constant tool, while at the same time books, plays, and poems have been banned because of words. Banning words also targets history leaving only select narratives for young people to learn only a narrow part of our country's history. Often these remaining narratives are missing the horrific parts of our country's history, which involve the harmful treatment of other people, such as Indigenous Americans or African Americans. Justification includes either not wanting young people to know this history or to feel bad about what happened. However, this only leads to the common saying that if we fail to learn from history, we are destined to repeat it.

Justice Ketanji Brown Jackson shared the following on September 12, 2023, as the keynote speaker at the 60th anniversary of the Ku Klux Klan bombing that killed four young girls at the Sixteenth Street Baptist Church in Birmingham, Alabama:

> There was a reason that my parents felt it was important to introduce me to those uncomfortable topics and it was not to make me feel like a victim or crush my spirits. To the contrary, my parents understood that I had to know those hard truths in order to expand my horizons. They understood that we can only know where we are and where we're going, if we realize where we've been. Knowledge of the past is what enables us to mark our forward progress.

> If we're going to continue to move forward as a nation we cannot allow concerns about discomfort to displace knowledge, truth or history. I know that atrocities like the one we're memorializing today are difficult to remember and relive. But I also know that it is dangerous to forget them. It is certainly the case that parts of this country's story can be hard to think about. We cannot forget because the uncomfortable lessons are often the ones that teach us the most about ourselves. We cannot forget because we cannot learn from past mistakes we do not know exist.
>
> … So yes, learning about our country's history can be painful, but history is also our best teacher. Yes, our past is filled with too much violence, too much hatred, too much prejudice. But can we really say that we are not confronting those same evils now?
>
> (Jackson, 2023, pp. 11–12)

Included in Inaugural Youth Poet Laureate Amanda Gorman's poem, *The Hill We Climb*, is the line, "For while we have our eyes on the future, history has its eyes on us" (Gorman, 2021, p. 21). This poem has also been the target of those that want to ban words and silence ideas that make them uncomfortable or do not align to their views. It is no coincidence that many of the works being silenced are by authors of color or part of the LGBTQ+ community. This is history repeating itself and silence is what *Giving Voice* strives to shatter. The needed conversations can be the most difficult to have. These are the conversations that transform the people who have them. It is very difficult work for audience members, for troupe members, and for troupe leaders.

We let our audience know that ignoring an oppression is the most common tactic used when faced with oppression. It is used by people of all ages and walks of life. They remain silent. The silence may be out of ignorance, not knowing what to do or it may be out of fear, of doing the wrong thing. However, silence indicates approval. Most of our audience members do not approve of microaggressions and realize they need to start addressing oppression rather than pretending they did not hear or see something oppressive. Our overall goal is for the audience members to not only become aware but be empowered to act, to speak up and to make their own environments a safer place for everyone.

It would be easy to lament all the challenges, including the same oppressions happening over and over. It is also easy to get stuck looking at where we are and how far we still need to go. This is when you remind your troupe and, possibly, yourself how far we have come. As Dr. Martin Luther King, Jr. said in his speech at the Washington National Cathedral, "We shall overcome because the arc of the moral universe is long, but it bends toward justice" (King, 1968).

Boal developed this type of theatre for people to rehearse being the protagonist of their own lives. People become part of improving the scenario, part of the solution, rather than sitting back silently and watching oppression happen, sometimes again and again. It is a safe yet powerful way to examine life's challenges and try ideas to make life better. Hopefully, more troupes will continue to develop and give voice to those silenced and marginalized. This is how the difficult but courageous conversations can begin. "Theatre is a form of knowledge: it should and can also be a means of transforming society. Theatre can help us build our future, rather than just waiting for it" (Boal, 1992, p.16). As long as there are those willing to no longer be silent, but instead use their own voice for the greater good, there is hope. As stated by Boal, it is "rehearsal for life."

References

Boal, A. (1992). *Games for actors and non-actors* (A. Jackson, Trans.). Routledge.

Gorman, A. (2021). *The hill we climb*. Viking Books

Jackson, K. (2023, September 15). *Commemorate and mourn, celebrate and warn*. Supreme Court of the United States. Retrived December 18, 2023, from https://www.supremecourt.gov/publicinfo/speeches/Justice_Jackson_Sixteenth_Street_Baptist_Church_Speech.pdf

King, M. L. (1964). *Strength to love* (1st ed.). Pocket Book Edition.

King, M. L. (1968, March 31). *Quotations*. Martin Luther King, Jr., Memorial. NPS. https://www.nps.gov/mlkm/learn/quotations.htm#:~:text=%22We%20shall%20overcome%20because%20the,Cathedral%2C%20March%2031%2C%201968.

Index

For Product Safety Concerns and Information please contact our EU representative GPSR@taylorandfrancis.com
Taylor & Francis Verlag GmbH, Kaufingerstraße 24, 80331 München, Germany

www.ingramcontent.com/pod-product-compliance
Lightning Source LLC
LaVergne TN
LVHW010924110826
845149LV00013B/2471